Mr. *Hold-the-World*. Ay, and hold you there still, good Mr. *By-ends*; for, for my part, I can count him but a Fool, that having the Liberty to keep what he has, shall be so unwise as to lose it. Let us be wise *as Serpents*; it's best to make hay when the Sun shines; you see how the Bee lieth still all winter, and bestirs her only when she can have Profit with Pleasure. God sends sometimes rain, and sometimes sun-shine: If they be such fools to go through the first, yet let us be content to take fair weather along with us. For my part, I like that Religion best, that will stand with the security of God's good blessings unto us: For who can imagine, that is ruled by his Reason, since God has bestowed upon us the good things of this Life, but that he would have us keep them for his Sake. *Abraham* and *Solomon* grew rich in Religion. And *Job* says, That a good man *shall lay up Gold as Dust.*

The Pilgrim's Progress

Samuel Butler Revalued

THOMAS L. JEFFERS

THE PENNSYLVANIA STATE UNIVERSITY PRESS
UNIVERSITY PARK AND LONDON

Publication of this book was aided by a grant from the Hull Memorial Publication Fund of Cornell University.

Library of Congress Cataloging in Publication Data

Jeffers, Thomas L.   1946–
    Includes bibliography and index.
    1.   Butler, Samuel, 1835-1902—Criticism and interpre-
tation.   I.   Title.
PR4349.B7Z776   823'.809   80-24904
ISBN 0-271-00281-6

Designed by DOLLY CARR

Printed in the United States of America

For Pauli, Matthew, and Adam

Contents

Introduction

This is a study in revaluation. Thanks to Clara G. Stillman,[1] Samuel
Butler has long been recognized as an early exponent of ideas which
certain twentieth-century writers, from Bergson to Whitehead to
Freud, either wittingly borrowed or unwittingly reconceived. While
not neglecting this line of study, I believe that it has given the
unwarranted impression that Butler was a lonely seer, a studious
eccentric who exhumed and galvanized the ideas of forgotten
theorists like Lamarck and turned them against the deep-rooted
intellectual establishment of the late Victorian Age. This is to mistake his social position — that of a man whose genius was hidden
under his cloak as, from his rooms at Clifford's Inn, he scurried under
the dome of the British Museum, and whose literary reputation had
flashed but once, and then only because the public thought the
anonymous author of the first edition of *Erewhon* might be Lord
Lytton — for his spiritual position. His writings teem with ideas
which are continuous with the pre-Victorian tradition of liber-
tarianism in education, hedonism in ethics, and a sort of reverent
agnosticism in natural theology. Writers such as Locke, Hume, Dr.
Johnson, Lord Chesterfield, and William Cobbett helped variously to
create and apply the philosophical assumptions which Butler found
at hand when he needed a grounding different from his father's
Pauline Christianity and public school "hypothetics," just as he
himself went on to develop assumptions which Shaw, Forster, Virginia Woolf and others would have at hand in their different times of
need.

I am not concerned with influence in the usual sense. Butler was
very scrupulous about citing sources; indeed he knew he couldn't

think at all without borrowing, digesting, and transforming other people's ideas. He wanted to think *for* himself, but never *by* himself. The people whom he explicitly acknowledges as sources, however, are desolately few: Homer, Aristophanes, Shakespeare, Handel, Gibbon, Lamarck, and for a while Darwin. Other names crop up in his diversified *oeuvre* and in his notebooks, but with no particular concentrations. He read widely enough, so it is reasonable to suppose that if he took in Bishops Berkeley and Butler, then he also took in Locke and Hume; if Gibbon, then also Chesterfield. Hume in fact is mentioned several times, but there is little evidence to suggest that Butler had read him or any of my pre-Victorian examplars with much care. The fact is that once he began thinking for himself, he either obliterated his sources by surpassing them, as a normal human embryo obliterates its gill pouches, or assimilated and turned them to his own uses, as the species in general has done with the legacy got from the lemur — the opposable first digit on its hand. In short, his sources became unconscious, his memory of them being more nervous than rational. This is precisely the sort of influence Butler was most interested in. In intellectual as in physiological affairs, certain creatures establish the conditions which those who come after must willy-nilly live under. They may alter the conditions — indeed in small ways they probably will — but they can't altogether escape them. To be sure, any number of writers established the conditions under which Butler had to begin his work, and one might well consider how Paul, Augustine, Bunyan, Fielding, Burke, Bentham, Hazlitt, or Disraeli helped determine the ends and means of his genius. But I hope to demonstrate that the pre-Victorians I have focused on are, more specially than others, what Borges would call Butler's *created* precursors.[2] The demonstration stands or falls, of course, on whether we shall see Butler more vividly by regarding him as following out of them, and them more vividly as leading up to him. Not that he is the terminus. Rather, he is a great mediator — a probing entrepreneur, an inspired mountebank, and a creative novelist — who in his turn has had a traceable influence, conscious and unconscious both. Along the continuum of ideas there is a conscious strain we can document from, say, Gibbon to Butler to Forster; and there is an unconscious one we can divine from, say, Hume to Butler to someone like Angus Wilson. Inquiries in the latter strain can be as fruitful as those in the former. To anyone who, for example, understood both the fossil record and geological history, the linkage between reptiles and birds was as much a compelling

article of evolutionary faith before the discovery of the archaeopteryx as it was after.

I have assumed an acquaintance with the two Butlerian texts that
have remained in print throughout this century, *Erewhon* and, more
especially, *The Way of All Flesh*, and at moments I have glanced at the
particulars of the life in a manner that presupposes an acquaintance
with Henderson's if not with Jones's biography. To stir the reader's
memory of these matters, though, I offer the following brief summary
of the salient facts of Butler's career.

He was born in 1835 at Langar Rectory in Nottinghamshire, the son
of the Reverend (and later Canon) Thomas Butler, and the grandson
of Dr. Samuel Butler, headmaster of Shrewsbury School, which
Charles Darwin attended, and eventually Bishop of Lichfield and
Coventry. The family money made possible a marvelous trip to the
Continent in 1843 which initiated Butler's lifelong enthusiasm for
Italy, but it also made inevitable the circuit of Shrewsbury School
and St. John's College, Cambridge, for which he felt guiltily ungrateful. He was being prepared for ordination, but in 1859, assailed
by specific doubts as to infant baptism and by very general doubts as
to his temperamental fitness for the cloth, he rebelled. After a hope-
less epistolary discussion with Langar — Butler wanting to study
painting, his father wanting him, if he *would* not be ordained, to
study law — it was agreed that he should emigrate. He sailed to New
Zealand, where for four years — he wanted to be a real pastor — he
herded sheep. He would be gone, he thought, "some ten or dozen
years." "It shall be my constant endeavour," he wrote his parents
from Cambridge, "to make you both feel that in consenting to my
departure for a considerable time, you will have rather gained a son
than lost one.... Wednesday will be the 10th. Can I leave on the
following Monday?"[3] Aided by a large sum of capital put up by his
father, Butler turned his sheep-run into so profitable a venture that
he was able to return to England in 1864 and live off his dividends.
He studied painting, for which he had but meagre talent, at Heatherley's Art School, and took rooms at Clifford's Inn, where he lived
the rest of his life.

New Zealand had not been all sheep ranching. Butler had kept up
his passion for music, playing Bach and Handel every night on an
organ he had had carted up from Christchurch. More important, he
had kept up his reading. He had gone through Gibbon during the
voyage down under, and had felt the foundations of Christian orthodoxy trembling. Once on land, he read Darwin as though *The*

Origin were a new Bible, and, looking up, he saw the foundations strewn round him. His real start as a writer came with "Darwin Among the Machines" and other *jeux d'espirit* which he published in the New Zealand *Press*, and which he recast half a decade later as parts of *Erewhon*, brought out anonymously in 1872, and under his own name in a second edition the same year. Angry at this bit of published irreverence, Canon Butler forbade his son to visit Langar, but when in 1873 Mrs. Butler lay dying, he called the prodigal to her bed in Menton, France, and there accused him of having killed her with the book.

Stimulated by this paternal insult, Butler returned to London and began *The Way of All Flesh*, which he was to continue to work on sporadically till 1884. He always intended to rewrite the last third, but the MS. stayed locked in his drawer, as V.S. Pritchett has said, waiting like a time bomb "to blow up the Victorian family and with it the whole great pillared and balustraded edifice of the Victorian novel."[4] It was published in 1903, the year after Butler's death. In 1873 he wrote *The Fair Haven*, an ironic defense of belief in Christian miracles put forward by "John Pickard Owen." It builds on the anonymous pamphlet, "The Evidence for the Resurrection of Jesus Christ as contained in the Four Evangelists critically examined," which Butler had published privately in 1865, and which addresses the inconsistencies of the Gospel accounts. His intention in *The Fair Haven* was to show up the sophistries of Christian apologetics, but so skillfully did he mime them that early reviewers hailed the book as a defense of the faith. When they discovered that it came from the pen of the author of *Erewhon*, they determined, understandably, not to touch him again: they didn't want to be embarrassed twice. The book also included an introductory memoir by "W.B. Owen," in which Butler's adeptness as a historian of life in an Evangelical family is evident. Next came *Life and Habit* (1877), which is the first and best of a series of books — *Evolution Old and New* (1879), *Unconscious Memory* (1880), and *Luck, or Cunning, as the main means of organic modification?* (1887) — quarreling not with evolution as such, but with Darwin's theory of natural selection. Butler also wrote a superbly idiosyncratic travel book, *Alps and Sanctuaries* (1881), which has something of a Baedeker and something of D. H. Lawrence's *Twilight in Italy*; *The Authoress of the Odyssey* (1897), which persuasively argues that "Nausicaa" composed the poem, using places along the coast of Sicily as sites for Odysseus' adventures; vigorously idiomatic translations of *The Iliad* (1898) and *The Odyssey* (1900); *Shake-*

speare's *Sonnets Reconsidered and in part rearranged* (1899), a nig-
gling book which has received deservedly less attention than Oscar
Wilde's similar thesis about Shakespeare's youthful friendship with
"Mr. W. H."; and *Erewhon Revisited* (1901), which adds little to the
oeuvre's store of ideas, but which is nonetheless a witty and surpris-
ingly warm production. Besides this incomplete list, there are two
volumes of essays, several of which still make provocative reading,
and the posthumously published and widely appreciated *Notebooks*
(1912), which contain the vigorous seeds of his public utterances.

Four people were important to Butler in his lifetime. The chief
among them was his father, a reasonably full picture of whom can be
pieced together between *The Way of All Flesh* and *The Family Letters*,
the resemblance between Canon Butler and Theobald Pontifex being
close enough to nullify the early protests of people who had known
the family. Next was Charles Paine Pauli, the enigmatically sophisticated, frequently ill, and apparently penniless man whom Butler
met in New Zealand. As a latent or confused homosexual, Butler was
at any rate infatuated with Pauli. He brought him back to London
and, even in times when he himself could little afford it, gave him
regular financial assistance — some ₤6000 over thirty-two years! —
and more-than-weekly luncheons, an arrangement which continued
till Pauli died in 1897, when it transpired that the man had been
ignobly milking at least two other gentleman all along. It was Pauli
as Butler first thought him who went into the character of Towneley
in *The Way of All Flesh*. Next was Miss E. M. A. Savage, whom Butler
met at Heatherley's in 1867, and whom he might have married if she
had only been handsomer or somehow more alluring to his sexually
disabled taste. From her he got invaluable literary criticism and
encouragement. Finally there was Henry Festing Jones, his major
biographer, sixteen years his junior, whom he met in 1876. Jones was
the male companion, the familiar of Clifford's Inn, who both helped
sustain Butler emotionally and gave the Edwardians a living link
with the (to them) heroic author of *The Way of All Flesh*.

The process of revaluating Butler within the backward- and
forward-resonating tradition I have sketched at the beginning of this
introduction is in effect a process of rehabilitation. I think he de-
serves a more prominent place than he has had in the last sixty years
— since Henry Festing Jones's *Samuel Butler ... A Memoir* (London:
Macmillan, 1919) both consummated the posthumous glorification
and began the inevitable disillusionment. The nadir was reached by
Malcolm Muggeridge's sneering *The Earnest Atheist* (London: Eyre &

Spottiswoode, 1936). P. N. Furbank, in his brief *Samuel Butler* (Cambridge, Eng.: Cambridge University Press, 1948), rendered unto Muggeridge what was Muggeridge's, sifted through the memorabilia that had surfaced since Jones, and gave Butler the uncommonly subtle and yet generous psychological reading which had hitherto been lacking. Since then, in spite of Philip Henderson's smooth biography, *Samuel Butler: The Incarnate Bachelor* (London: Cohen & West, 1953), Basil Willey's acute but incomplete *Butler and Darwin: Two Versions of Evolution* (New York: Harcourt, 1960), Arnold Silver's fine edition of *The Family Letters of Samuel Butler, 1841-1886* (Stanford: Stanford University Press, 1962), Daniel F. Howard's indispensible edition of *The Way of All Flesh* (Boston: Houghton Mifflin, 1964), and the inclusion of discussions of *The Way of All Flesh* in books on Victorian childhood or on religious humanism — to all of which I owe a debt — the study of Butler has fallen into desuetude or, worse, into clichéd misunderstanding. My specific corrections of these misunderstandings will come along the way, but I ought to say beforehand that what follows is no panegyric. We shouldn't blink at Butler's failings as a man and as a writer, but neither should we let them obscure his lively subtlety, his persistent questioning, or his earnest religiousness.

Though much of what Butler wrote in his books on art history, on Shakespeare, and on *The Odyssey* gets only slight mention here, I have tried to see his most famous book, *The Way of All Flesh,* as steadily and as wholly as possible. Because it is also the book whose composition (1873-84) spans the years in which Butler did his most creative thinking about Christianity, Darwinism, and his own family relations, *The Way of All Flesh* best brackets the evolution of Butler himself. It is the center round which I imagine not only his precursors and heirs, but *Erewhon, The Fair Haven, Life and Habit,* and the major essays to revolve. My first two chapters attend to what he thought of as the deconstructing of his forebears' religion and the constructing of his own. My third is about the ethical, and my fourth and fifth about the educational corollaries to that religion. In my last chapter I endeavor to place Butler fairly as a novelist and as a polemicist — to answer his critics (and his lauders) without granting or claiming too much. Throughout, my concern is to determine the possibilities for looking on him as someone who is after all a living author, able still both to vivify us and to make us patient.

I wish to thank David Wee of St. Olaf College, who first got me to read *The Way of All Flesh*; Paul Holmer of Yale Divinity School, who, while he wouldn't at all approve of Butler's kind of religiosity, did impress me with the possibility of there being more to "the grammar of faith" than is apparent among the Battersby Christians; and J. Hillis Miller and Charles Feidelson, Jr., both of Yale, who encouraged me through a dissertation chapter on Butler which is the dimly remembered hamlet buried beneath this book. A compressed and slightly revised version of that dissertation chapter was published in the *Samuel Butler Newsletter*, vol. 2, no. 2 (1979), from which, with permission, I have taken some dozen sentences. Finally, I want to express my appreciation to two Cornellians: Mary Adesso, secretary in the English Department, who quickly and cleanly typed the bulk of the MS.; and Dr. Howard Evans, head of the Anatomy Department in the Veterinary School, who, during all the rides he gave me home from campus, would talk to me about the pterodactyl and the archaeopteryx.

1

The Demythology

Locke argued that all our notions about the universe are based on post-natal experience. With a boldness greater than Locke's, Hume pursued this thesis into the regions of ethics and theology, which, like physics, astronomy, or any other branch of "natural philosophy," should be "founded on fact and observation."[1] However piously one might worship the Maker of heaven and earth, Hume says, one must admit to having had direct observation neither of the making in question, nor of any particular providence intervening to sustain what was made. Therefore no *a posteriori* proof of God's existence is possible, and no version of *a priori* proof, which says that heaven and earth must have a cause like everything else, can silence the question of the cause of that cause. One gets not a demonstrated and knowable First Cause, but an infinite regress of causes.

Burdened with the inefficacy of both inductive and deductive reason, Hume is not, however, completely smothered in a cloud of unknowing. When he anatomizes the eye, or when he enumerates the excellences of the hand, "the suppleness and variety of [the] joints," he feels "the idea of a contriver...immediately flow in upon [him] with a force like that of sensation."[2] Though from reason he draws a blank, from sentiment he discovers a teleology. Still, the products of this discovery are theologically minimal and ethically barren. He can affirm at most the "one simple, though somewhat ambiguous, at least undefined proposition, *that the cause or causes of order in the universe bear some remote analogy to human intelligence*" — a proposition as useless as it is uncertain, for it affords no inference about how we should conduct ourselves, or about the deity's moral attributes, whether of "infinite benevolence," "infinite power," or "infinite wisdom."[3]

Hume approvingly paraphrases Bacon's dictum that *"A little philosophy...makes men atheists: a great deal reconciles them to religion."*[4] Samuel Butler would agree, even though it was Bacon who said it. Indeed he would go further, for Hume justifies the dictum only to the extent of giving "plain, philosophical assent" to the statement that an intelligent *"cause or causes"* exist. Butler is more confident than Hume of our ability to draw inferences about God's moral attributes from our observation of natural phenomena, since of all the possible divine causes of the universe, the one that concerns us is not external to it — a Maker beyond space-time, and thus beyond our apprehension — but subsistent within it, manifest in the shrewd *making* which Darwin taught him to call evolution. Butler's reconciliation to religion, however, is the subject of my second chapter — a subject we ought to approach only after having traced the double processes of his reaction against the religion of his forebears. The first process is intellectual, the second filial.

I

In his essay "Of Miracles," Hume shows how an empiricist should approach religious stories by trying to differentiate the historical fact from the apocryphal legend. Finding precious little fact, he concludes that there is nothing in religion for anyone but the ignorant and the barbarous. That is Butler's initial conclusion, in the feverish excitement of discovering that everyone from his father to his tutor has leagued to tell him that legend isn't legend at all. At last he can throw off what Carlyle, in "Shooting Niagara," characteristically dubbed the "Hebrew old clothes" of orthodox superstition! After the excitement, however, he settles down to inquire whether the Hebrew and early Christian legends might shroud something significant. As Mill would say, he doesn't ask simply the Benthamite question "Is it true?" — true in the way propositions in mathematics or physics are true; like David Friedrich Strauss, or like Strauss's translator George Eliot, he asks the Coleridgean question "What does it mean?" Why should men ever have felt the need to believe *that*, whether the story of the resurrection or the dogma of the Athanasian creed? If "apocrypha" comes from *apokruptein* (to hide away), what is, or at least may be "hidden" in these now-broadened *scripta apocrypha*?[5] The religious truths which may be there will no doubt be difficult for ordinary men to understand, just as mathematical or scientific truths often are. But they can be made more accessible by being disengaged from accompanying fictions disguised as facts, or by being read in a key different from their narrative medium. As Bernard Shaw says, "...no student of science has yet been taught that specific gravity consists in the belief that Archimedes jumped out of his bath and ran naked through the streets of Syracuse shouting Eureka, Eureka, or that the law of inverse squares must be discarded if anyone can prove that Newton was never in an orchard in his life."[6] Similarly, the truth of the story of Christ's resurrection doesn't depend upon a belief in a great earthquake, in a descent of an angel with a countenance like lightning, and in a foot-race between John and Peter.

In The Way of All Flesh Theobald Pontifex is being asked, as a clergyman, to believe that these adventitious details are integral to the truth of the story, when actually the details are inconsistently various in the four gospel texts, just as several accounts of any event would be. Not that Theobald worries or even knows about the variances of the texts. His is the larger problem of having to do business according to a belief in the miraculous, viewing the unbounded universe of the nineteenth century as though it were the three-tiered universe of the sixteenth, wherein the dead come to life again, some going up to the top tier, others going down, now on the basis of sublime criteria such as whether they have loved their neighbor, now on the basis of vulgar criteria such as whether they have abstained from blood puddings — all of which he must uphold as a barrister does his client's alibi: because he is paid to. He dare not consider the other side of the story — that, historically, Christ never died on the cross at all, or that, religiously, the legend that he did so die and rise again may mean something about the will of life to renew itself, not only in spite of those who prefer Barabbas, but in spite of ice ages, diseases, and civil wars. If Theobald were to consider this sort of reading, he would no longer be able to entrench himself behind the Thirty-nine Articles whenever a parishioner wailed out his or her fears of eternal damnation. But as it is, he has got to be dishonest, and worse, to be so without knowing it.

His son Ernest can better afford to be honest, but nothing happens at Roughborough or Cambridge to enable him to be. The schools have a financial stake in the Church of England and are loath to trouble what they take to be its foundation.[7] This is what one might expect. If a man has a bad ten-pound note, he will naturally refuse to look at the evidence against it; he wants the note to be able to purchase what it says it can. But if the note weren't his, he would see at once that it is bad.[8] The story of the resurrection is a bad note that has been given to Ernest, as to his father and forefathers. Mr. Shaw the tinker asks him to look at the note as if it belonged to someone else — i.e., to read the four accounts in the gospels "not as wanting to find the story true but as wanting to find out whether it is true or not." After an hour, the "No" which God has directed to sinful man is turned back trebly onto the pages of the book about God, "and in respect of the most important of all the events which are recorded in it."[9] As Hume pointedly declares: "When anyone tells me that he saw a dead man restored to life, I immediately consider with myself whether it be more probable that this person should either deceive or be deceived, or that the fact which he relates should really have happened."[10] When Ernest finds how much the witnesses differ — let us put aside his naive expectations about what degree of consistency historical documents ought to have — he thinks the presumption is decidedly against the truth of the miracle they claim to recount. Henceforth, asking him to believe the story of the resurrection is like Theobald's asking him, when he was three or four years old, to say "come" when the best his tongue could do was "tum." It is to try to contradict the way bodies work.

II

So much for the surface of the intellectual rebellion against Christianity which Butler repeats through his novel about Ernest Pontifex. That an elementary problem in Form Criticism should be enough to revolutionize Ernest's thinking about his faith suggests not only that he has done very little thinking about it at all, but also that he has been prepared for such a revolution by having been, in Mr. Shaw the tinker's words, "real bad brought up." Any intellectual case against Christianity will serve because the filial case against it — the case learned through years of being the first-born in what passes among his neighbors as a Christian household — is so complete. All the anxiety that Christina feels about having eaten blood puddings, and that Theobald feels about his ineptitude with sick sinners who can't face an eternity of torture with more indifference, is projected onto their children. As Lloyd deMause has said, "The use of the child as a 'toilet' for adult projections is behind the whole notion of original sin...."[11] That is too reductive, of course: man's sense of originary separation from God — his sense of ontological inferiority, as it were — is "behind the whole notion" also. But parental anxiety projected onto children certainly aggravates the ontological inferiority which the latter are suffering from enough as it is. The author of the Church catechism obviously neglected to consult any children while he was writing, nor does he appear to have liked them. Indeed, "The general impression it [the catechism] leaves upon the mind of the young is that their wickedness at birth was but very imperfectly wiped out at baptism and that the mere fact of being young at all has something with it that savours more or less distinctly of the nature of sin" (WAF, 30). By the nineteenth century this Puritanically Christian view of children had been eroded by the Lockean view, which effectually denied that children were wicked at birth, since at birth they were merely tablets with nothing, wicked or otherwise, yet written on them. Theirs is the innocence of ignorance. But this view, which is not to be confused with the Romantics' belief that the infant tablet is sacredly inscribed, was still too often overshadowed by the Puritan conviction that every person must relive the history of the race as a whole. Infants may start out innocent, like Adam and Eve, but their Eden is, in J. H. Plumb's words, "surrounded by serpents and cluttered with apples." In spite of parental vigilance, children are doomed to repeat man's first disobedience.[12] As Christina exclaims in what she expects will be her final reassuring message to her sons, "you will — you must fall" (WAF, 94). She intends that as a warning against their trusting in themselves instead of in God, but like Raphael's similar warning in Paradise Lost, it sounds like a resigned prophecy.

Small wonder that parents feel like a disappointed Jehovah, who created man only to see him turn out obstinate, stupid, and rebellious. Yet parents can solace themselves in the idea that their children are born for their benefit. We needn't go immediately to the Bible to discover early examples of this idea. One of several sources of Medea's grief in killing her children is that they won't be there to look after her when she gets old and to lay her out when she dies, but of course the selfish pleasure of revenging herself on Jason overcomes the selfish grief over what it will cost her.[13] The tenor of Medea's apology is a version of the ancients' usual apology for their widespread practice of infanticide. Though Seneca speaks of it as an act of mercy toward illegitimate or deformed children who would otherwise grow up painfully disadvantaged, the parents' common motive was solicitude for themselves: if an infant was inconvenient to them, they would expose it — especially if it was that very economically inconvenient thing, a girl.[14] But Puritan Christianity, following the lead of the Old Testament, seems to have perfected the theory of the child-as-convenience. Butler remarks how the theory

was so unanimously accepted in seventeenth-century England that
even Handel could sense nothing perverse in Milton's depiction of
Manoah's attitude toward Samson. In the air "How willing my
paternal love," Manoah

> tells us how good he is, and how little Samson really has to
> suffer in being blind — inasmuch as he, Manoah, can see
> perfectly well. This, he avers, should be enough for Samson:
> "Though wandering in the shades of night
> While *I* have eyes, *he* needs no light."
> Exactly so: this is the British parent theory all over. No
> wonder Milton's daughters did not like him. (*WAF,* 143–44.
> The couplet is from the pen of Handel's librettist, Newburgh
> Hamilton, but the sentiment is faithfully Miltonic.)

Manoah is only a more garrulous, less violent descendant of Medea,
from whom the child Samson would have done well to wiggle away
as soon as he could, and toward whom the grown-up Samson would
do well to be less submissive. As a latter-day Roundhead Samson,
Ernest has got to struggle for his own eyes in order to walk in his own
light, and to do it he must topple not only the temple of the Philis-
tines, but the rectory of his father.

The agon between father and son is physical as well as spiritual.
Theobald knows this from the start, construing his sister Alethaea's
interest in Ernest as a Byzantine plot: the boy should have no "allies"
(*WAF,* 124). Ernest eventually realizes he *needs* allies, whether it be
the coachman John, who threatens to break every bone in Theobald's
skin if he lays a hand on Ernest for having helped the unfortunate
Ellen; or the other boys at Roughborough, whom he joins in burning
his "governour"'s effigy on Guy Fawkes Day. This entire campaign,
beginning with the punishment for helping Ellen and the inquisition about the crimes of the boys at school, marks the time when
Ernest begins to acknowledge a warm dislike for both his parents,
especially his father, which, Butler adds, "means that he was now
beginning to be aware that he was reaching man's estate" (*WAF,* 160).
That is, father and son are less and less differentiable: they are man
and man exchanging gestures of similar dislike, each thinking the
other has given the original offense. As Theobald communes with
himself: "He's not fond of me; I'm sure he is not. He ought to be after
all the trouble I have taken with him, but he is ungrateful and selfish.
It is an unnatural thing for a boy not to be fond of his own father. If he

was fond of me I should be fond of him, but I cannot like a son who, I am sure, dislikes me" (WAF, 108). He already considers Ernest to have reached man's estate, inasmuch as the boy is acting not like a son but like a rival. Ernest therefore simply catches up with Theobald when he behaves with consciously unfilial enmity toward him. It is as though Samson had rejected the pious, parent-approved confession "I am a creature of my father," in favor of the declaration "I am a creature like my father."[15]

The possibility that father and son can become doubles of one another, imposing identical threats and justifying themselves with theologies which are either identical or mutually parodic, gives rise to Butler's several reversals of father-son relations in the Old Testament. Theobald, for instance, doubts the efficacy of the tenth plague on Egypt, for "if the little Egyptians had been anything like Ernest," the big Egyptians weren't likely to have traded the Israelites for them (WAF, 108). A father may easily wish his son dead, but a son may as easily return the wish, and even be willing to let his work force go free in order to make it come true. What got the Egyptians to "let the Jews go," Butler writes, "was an eleventh plague in consequence of which their papas and mammas were endowed with immortality" (my italics). Or to take another Old Testament family romance, it is attractive to imagine Isaac trying to sacrifice Abraham. But no matter how clearly the young man may have heard the divine call, his attempt will seem doubly "wrong." First, just as the little Egyptians were helpless before their fathers, so Isaac would be before his: "Fancy Abraham letting Isaac get him on to the mountain on such a ridiculous pretence as this [that God had told him to]!"[16] And second, Isaac would be too priggish to kick against the paternal will. Butler ponders a dialogue between Isaac and Ishmael on the night the former has returned from Moriah: "The rebellious Ishmael tries to stir up Isaac, and that good young man explains the righteousness of the transaction — without much effect" (N, 233). The distance between Isaac and his father is enough to guarantee that filial pieties will be observed. Between Ishmael and his father, however, the distance has broken down: closer in age, they have similar strength of body and similar independence of mind. "The war of extermination is generally fiercest between the most nearly allied species, for these stand most in one another's light" (N, 177). Should Abraham and Ishmael ever go up a mountain, they will both carry knives.

It is hard to say what the otherwise reliable Claude Bissell is thinking of when he says that Butler sought in evolutionary terms the God he had known in the "intimate, sympathetic, encompassing world of his childhood."[17] Rather, he sought the God whom he should have known then, but didn't. A child gets his ideas about God from his parents, and all is well, Butler avers, if only the parents have

> a genuine desire...to make the child feel that he is loved, and his natural feelings are respected....So soul-satisfying is family affection to a child, that he who has once enjoyed it cannot bear to be deprived of the hope that he is possessed in Heaven of a parent who is like his earthly father — of a friend and counsellor who will never, never fail him.[18]

A friend and counsellor, someone like the genial Reverend Mr. Irwine in *Adam Bede*: that is precisely the sort of man Theobald's background prevents him from being. The God he shadows forth is a "bald," flat, unimaginative despot who condemns smoking, drinking, swearing, and those "more delicate" schoolboy offenses which Ernest's fainting fit keeps him from confessing; a despot who will judge the quick and the dead in a magnified version of those inquisitions held in Battersby dining room. Any deity who is not an utter swindle should give his worshippers present nourishment. That is the obvious point of the several alimentary metaphors which Butler either invents or borrows from the Bible. He likens the Pontifexes' routine of morning and evening prayers to the quest of the bees who frequent the dining room when the windows are open in the summer, going from rose to rose on the wallpaper, sofa to ceiling and back again, never figuring out that though "so many of the associated ideas [are] present," "the main idea" — nectar — is missing "hopelessly and forever." Or there is Ernest staring fretfully at the painting of "Elijah or Elisha (whichever it was)," with the bread- and meat-carrying ravens in one corner, and the hungry prophet in another, till to comfort himself as well as Elijah he climbs up with a piece of bread and butter to trace a greasy diagonal from the ravens to the prophet's mouth. Finally, during his curacy Ernest angers the bishop but amuses the congregation by preaching *ex tempore* about "What kind of little cake it was that the widow of Sarepta had intended making when Elijah found her gathering a few sticks. He demonstrated that it was a seed cake" (*WAF*, 88, 155–56). Ernest homes toward that episode (I Kings 17:8–16) because it is one of those rare times when a biblical prophet is said to eat well: the widow "went and did according to the saying of Elijah: and she, and he, and her house, did eat many days. And the barrel of meal wasted not, neither did the cruse of oil fail...." Most of the time the food associated with prophets is either invisible, sparse, or unpalatable. Because they weren't prodigal, nobody killed the fatted calf for them. That, presumably, is why the lions wouldn't eat Daniel: "They could eat most things, but they drew the line at prophets."[19]

III

If, like the lions, Ernest desires what is savory and nourishing, why should he, the happy occupant of a room of his own at Cambridge, the bruited author of an iconoclastic essay on the Greek tragedians, suddenly begin to imitate Daniel? Why is he drawn to the Simeonites, the evangelical group of students who inhabit the catacombs of St. John's and who are epitomized by Badcock, "ugly, dirty, ill-dressed, bumptious," and deformed in a way which makes him waddle when he walks? It is because Ernest feels "instinctively that the Sims were after all much more like the early Christians than he was himself," and because, like Saul, he is convertible: he wants to stop persecuting and to begin emulating those who follow Christ (*WAF*, 190–91).

But which Christ? There is the unpleasant one manifested by the Simeonites — ascetic, unhandsome, hideously crucified, with whom broken people like Badcock identify and to whom the broken part of Ernest (which, after Theobald and Christina, would be the larger part) is naturally attracted. One is reminded of the remark of a Kingsley Amis character who has been beckoned to contemplate a crucifix: "You'll never get me up on one of those things!" Ernest, at first, *is* inclined to get up on one of those things, and looking back at this phase from the happier ending of a novel, one can see that the Christ whom he is following is the "false" one, a poison which must be purged from him — which Butler must purge from himself. Hence the exaggerated irreverence of his wish to have been among those who crucified Christ: "...but one must beware of spiritual pride. Who knows but what he himself might have been an apostle if temptation had fallen in his way?" Hence again the low humor with which he marks the sexual nullity of the Simeonites by giving Badcock his name, or the relentlessness with which he pursues his sister May, the "human Good Friday" preceding their father, the "human Sunday."[20] This purgative violence is trying to clear a path for the "true" Christ who is of course the antithesis of the crucified — the ambulatory, pleasant, kindly figure whom Butler purports to find, say, in Luke or in the unself-conscious art of the early Church, but whom he admits to having deduced mainly from his own ideas of what constitutes divinity. There doesn't have to be a textually ascertainable, historically fixable "true" Christ.[21] All the religious person needs is an instinct for what that embodiment of virtue would look like, if embodiment there need be. As Higgs, the Sunchild deified by the Erewhonian populace after his quite natural but to them miraculous ascension in a balloon, says when he returns twenty years later:

> ...if you cannot abolish me altogether, make me a peg on which to hang all your own best ethical and spiritual conceptions.... Sunchildism is still young and plastic; if you will let the cock-and-bull stories about me tacitly drop, and invent no new ones, beyond saying what a delightful person I was, I really cannot see why I should not do for you as well as any one else.[22]

The particular "peg" doesn't matter much, as long as the right "delightful" ideas are hung on it.

If one were to demythologize Christianity with the same intent one would Sunchildism, one would find that a good deal of adventitious material drops away, and that the revelation which Christ affords is of a man who is gentle, pleasant, and *nice*. The latter word, so perfunctory to us, has for Butler a manly and robust significance: it summarizes the qualities which conduce to our "truest and most lasting happiness." The essential *imitatio Christi*, therefore, is the eduction of all that is gentle and amiable in oneself. "He who takes the highest and most self-respecting view of his own welfare which it is in his power to conceive, and adheres to it in spite of conventionality, is a Christian whether he knows it and calls himself one, or whether he does not. A rose is not the less a rose because it does not know its own name" (*WAF*, 257). Therefore the injunction to give up all, even mother and father, for Christ's sake means to remove every obstacle to faring *well*, as one really understands that adverb oneself, not as conventional counsel understands it. This is a thoroughly "inner light" Christianity, a consequence of reading the Bible for a truth which one has inwardly but inarticulately defined beforehand. Butler secures his biblical truth by imperial redaction — cutting Acts 15:20, which is Christina's touchstone about "abstain[ing] from pollutions of idols, and from fornication, and from things strangled, and from blood"; but saving I Cor. 13, which is spiritually both interesting and vague enough to allow him to declare Christ a eudaemonist. The whole procedure will look villainously dishonest unless we grant Butler's premise that the text means very little beside the idea it is supposed to convey: it was plastically written, and it ought to be plastically read. Between the profession of and the denial of Christianity, he writes, "... it was a fight about names, not things; practically the Church of Rome, the Church of England, and the free-thinker have the same ideal standard and meet in the gentleman; for he is the most perfect saint who is the most perfect gentleman" (WAF, 260, my italics). If it is "a fight about names," then it must be waged with the weapons of names. The transvaluation of the name "Christ" comes not from mere prestidigitation, though Butler doesn't mind giving that impression. It comes from the often successful gamble that we can achieve apocalypse out of inversion. As Kenneth Burke would say, we can get a new and perhaps radical perspective on a word by looking at it in an incongruous way. Or in Butler's plain terms, we can give it a new currency value by "saying" it within a new "convention."[23]

Butler's most effective inversion is of the word "grace," which in the Latin forms of *gratia* (pleasure, favor, thanks) and *gratus* (favorable, pleasing) has a pre-theological stress which, in a theological climate, is worth rediscovering. We can best appreciate how well Butler does this by setting some of his statements next to analogous ones by Hume and Arnold. Butler writes of Paul among the Greeks:

> Grace! the old Pagan ideal whose charm even unlovely Paul could not withstand, but, as the legend tells us, his soul fainted within him, his heart misgave him, and standing alone on the seashore at dusk, he "troubled deaf heaven with his bootless cries," his thin voice pleading for grace after the flesh.
>
> The waves came in one after another, the seagulls cried together after their kind, the wind rustled among the dried canes upon the sandbanks, and there came a voice from heaven saying, "Let My grace be sufficient for thee." Whereon, failing of the thing itself, he stole the word and strove to crush its meaning to the measure of his own limitations. But the true grace, with her groves and high places, and troops of young men and maidens crowned with flowers, and singing of love and youth and wine — the true grace

> he drove out into the wilderness — high up, it may be, into
> Piora, and into such-like places. Happy they who harboured
> her in her ill report.[24]

The contrast between the Pauline and the Greek or Roman ideals is
traditional among British critics of popular Christianity. Hume pits
the classical hero against the Christian saint:

> *Brasidas* seized a mouse, and being bit by it, let it go. *There is
> nothing so contemptible, said he, but what may be safe, if it
> has but courage to defend itself.* Bellarmine patiently and
> humbly allowed the fleas and other odious vermin to prey
> upon him. *We shall have heaven, said he, to reward us for our
> sufferings: but these poor creatures have nothing but the en-
> joyment of the present life.* Such difference is there between
> the maxims of a *Greek* hero and a *Catholic* saint.[25]

Similarly, Arnold wonders what Virgil would have made of the
narrow intensity, the other-worldliness of even so venerable a group
as the Pilgrim Fathers:

> Notwithstanding the mighty results of the Pilgrim Fathers'
> voyage, they and their standard of perfection are rightly
> judged when we figure to ourselves Shakespeare or Virgil, —
> souls in whom sweetness and light, and all that in human
> nature is most humane, were eminent, — accompanying
> them on their voyage, and think what intolerable company
> Shakespeare and Virgil would have found them![26]

Though this passage from *Culture and Anarchy* is more well-known,
the anti-Hebraic statement which I shall quote next, and which
comes from Butler, is the more distinguished, for in it we get an irony
similar to Hume's, and superior to Arnold's in both concreteness and
corrosiveness. The passage is from *The Fair Haven*, where Butler
makes Owen descant upon the nobility of people like Bellarmine
whom, needless to say, Butler himself intensely dislikes:

> How infinitely nobler and more soul-satisfying is the ideal
> of the Christian saint with wasted limbs, and clothed in the
> garb of poverty — his upturned eyes piercing the very
> heavens in the ecstasy of a divine despair — than any of the

fleshly ideals of gross human conception such as [those of Phidias or Donatello]. . . . If a man does not feel this instinctively for himself, let him test it thus — whom does his heart of hearts tell him that his son will be most like God in resembling [note that the address is, so to speak, to Theobald on behalf of Ernest]? The Theseus? The Discobolus? or the St. Peters and St. Pauls of Guido and Domenichino? Who can hestitate for a moment as to which ideal presents the higher development of human nature? (FH, 230–31)

When the Theseus or the Discobolus is translated into the toff on Bond Street, Butler's admiration for the handsome, the athletic, and the dapper *can* seem like a sort of aesthetic Podsnappery:

People ask complainingly what swells have done, or do, for society that they should be able to live without working. The good swell is the creature towards which all nature has been groaning and travailing together until now. He is an ideal. He shows what may be done in the way of good breeding, health, looks, temper, and fortune. He realizes men's dreams of themselves, at any rate vicariously. He preaches the gospel of grace. The world is like a spoilt child, it has this good thing given it at great expense and then says it is useless! (N, 28–29)

Fortunately, though, more is behind a jotting like this than the envy of a Paul for the "young men and maidens crowned with flowers," or of a Guidoesque Peter for a Phidian decathlon champion. Butler's remarks about Hellenic and Hebraic ideals of human perfection have the astringency and the cogency they do because he thinks of "good breeding" as the *summum bonum* not just in the sense of the cultivation of a "grace of manner," but in the sense of a robust "continuance of the race" (N, 27). Good breeding is the labor of an intelligent Will which the toff best worships in his insouciance, but which the philosopher best worships, first, in the precise study of its abundant creations, the cat and the gentian as well as the human "good swell"; and second, in written defense of its cunning providence against those who calumniate it — not the Battersby Christians, after all, but those anti-religionists who still call *The Origin of Species* what the young Butler once called it: "the book."

2

The Religion

Ever since Augustine, as Basil Willey has pointed out in his eloquently succinct study of Butler and Darwin, there has been nothing incompatible between religion and evolution.[1] Augustine interprets the creation stories in Genesis as elaborated figures for how God infused the earth with the necessary energy to go on producing flora and fauna by natural processes. Since that beginning, God has appeared to rest from his work, but in fact he remains the animating spirit which impels all life to continue to adapt itself in ways that will enable it not merely to survive, but to flourish. Though one species suffers because another surpasses it, both are members one of another, both are parts of the creation which reveals the original goodness of the spirit that brooded over it. Augustine affirms something about the "why" as well as about the "how" of creation. The modern temper, scientific and historical in its emphases, has let the "why" question drop in its interest in the "how" and the "what."

Darwin saw in abundant detail the "what" of adaptive changes in the course of the earth's history, and in order to explain how those changes occur, he put forward the hypothesis of pangenesis, according to which all the cells in the body generate emissaries that enter the bloodstream and come together in the reproductive cells. The discovery of DNA has superseded the pangenetic hypothesis, and Butler would be as grateful as Darwin to learn about the chromosomal constituent of cell nuclei, spiralled and bonded in a manner that determines the characteristics a new creature will inherit. Butler's principal question, however, remains unanswered: we don't know *why* DNA performs its labors, nor *whence* it derives its power to do so. One cannot dismiss Butler, as George Gaylord Simpson does, by saying that he errs "in applying artistic methods and judgments to inappropriate fields," i.e., that he speaks of biological or chemical processes in terms of human intellectual processes.[2] The debate between Butler and Darwin is less methodological (what language shall we use to talk about evolution?) than metaphysical (what are the realities, material and otherwise, which are present in the "things" which evolve?). One can say with Charles Kingsley that "Mother Nature lets things make themselves";[3] that, say, the human species has made itself eyes which are superior in stereoscopy to those of birds. One can even reduce the mystery of how that adaptive marvel has been accomplished by tracing through fossils the eyes' gradual frontalization and narrowing. But why the species should have wanted to see stereoscopically at a glance instead of having, like a bird, to turn first one eye and then the other upon an object, or why indeed there is a species to see and a world of objects to be seen, instead of no species and no world, are all questions which the metaphysics implicit in Darwinism cannot legitimately ask, much less answer. They are pseudo-questions, just as attempts at answering them are pseudo-statements.

I

For Darwin there is no apprehensible cause in back of or goal in front of evolutionary change. Adaptations are simply fortuitous, the lucky accidents surviving because they are fit for the environment, the unlucky going to the wall. Butler agrees that luck is important, but if it were everything, he points out, the universe would be nothing more than what Darwin seems content with — the stupid product of random shots, with no design purposed within it. Like Carlyle, Butler cannot understand how men can find joy in the blankly mechanistic universe imaged forth by The Origin and its popularizers. They may feel relief in assuming that the claims of religion have collapsed before those of materialistic science, and that the wearing task of reconciling the two is over, but Butler thinks their exultation premature. The task is not over, and he determines to take it up anew, by searching not just for a truer sense of the religious, as we have seen, but for a truer sense of the scientific. He does both, of course, when he returns to Lamarck. It was the French naturalist's hypothesis that what immediately appears to be a matter of luck — e.g. it is lucky we can breathe above water — is more deeply a matter of cunning, the result of an act of will among pioneering amphibians who so determined, wanted, and invented the capacity to breathe the air, that their heirs have never again had to go to the water except to drink or cast nets. Exactly how such an adaptation initially occurred, and how it was transmitted to us, the fortunate heirs, is as unanswered a question for Butler as it is for Darwin. But the answers, when they come, will be meaningful, Butler insists, only if we have understood the reason for the adaptation in the first place: it is not a freakish accident which, because it happens to jibe with the creature's needs in a particular environment, proves essential to survival; it is an intelligent improvisation, a *making* in accordance with perceived needs.

Butler cannot prove that this Lamarckian hypothesis is correct, nor can a Huxley prove that the Darwinian one is. Both hypotheses account for the "what" of evolution, the data culled from fossils or from current observation of controlled or spontaneous variations. Choosing between the hypotheses is an act of faith — a Pascalian wager — as is evident from the ardently religious tone of the close of *Life and Habit*: "Will the reader bid me wake with him to a world of chance and blindness? Or can I persuade him to dream with me of a more living faith than either he or I had as yet conceived as possible? As I have said, reason points remorselessly to an awakening, but faith and hope still beckon to the dream" (*LH*, 250). Recalling the old teleologist argument that we can no more expect our patently ordered universe to come into being through the random play of atoms than we can expect a tremendous pot of alphabet noodles, spilling over again and again, to spill its contents at last into the ordered text of *The Winter's Tale*, Butler might say, with Shaw, "that mere survival of the fittest in the struggle for existence plus sexual selection fail [sic] as hopelessly to account for Darwin's own life work as for my conquest of [learning how to ride] the bicycle." Yet he must allow that there may be other material factors, so far "unnoticed or undiscovered," which could account for the evolution of an automatic Darwin or Shakespeare; or that given an indefinitely immense amount of time, the random aggregations of atoms might produce not only *The Winter's Tale* but St. Paul's ode to charity. He must allow these possibilities, and he must out of his own bowels deny them.

> When [in Shaw's words] a man tells you that you are a product of Circumstantial Selection solely, you cannot finally disprove it. You can only tell him out of the depths of your inner conviction that he is a fool and a liar. But as this,

though British, is uncivil, it is wiser to offer him the counter-assurance that you are the product of Lamarckian evolution...and challenge him to disprove *that,* which he can no more do than you can disprove Circumstantial Selection, both forces being conceivably able to produce anything if you only give them rope enough.[4]

Huxley and the positivists too glibly assert that they are justified not by faith but by verification. For even the verification procedure rests on a belief in the regularity and uniformity of nature, the accuracy of man's senses or of his instruments for observation, and so on. The creative evolutionist has the advantage of at least knowing himself to be back where, if he is a Butler or Shaw, he began: with St. Paul's justification by faith, a trust in an undemonstrable first premise which must be reverenced as dogma. As Butler rightly observes, even a mathematics as reflective of the experiential world as Euclidean geometry must begin dogmatically. Without "axioms which transcend demonstration," the geometrist can demonstrate nothing; with them, he can demonstrate a great deal. He shall live by faith, just like everyone else. Luther said, not in resignation but in defiance, "Here I stand, I can do no other"; similarly, if anyone hold out against Euclid, the latter can only call him a fool and pronounce his position "absurd" (N, 337). Stubbornness is the ultimate weapon.

We can follow Butler's early soundings for a faith in the often tipsy ironies of *Erewhon*'s "The Book of the Machines." Most readers can recognize the satire on men's dependence on machines, from elementary tools to steam engines, and on the enslaving amount of time they spend maintaining them, improving them for commercial or military struggle, etc. This Ruskin-Morris theme, however, is not the whole of Butler's intent, nor are the "Darwinian materials" merely by the way, as A. Dwight Culler thinks.[5] The Erewhonians' Luddite campaign is sensible insofar as they want to liberate themselves from the tyranny of a technology which rides upon *them,* but it is nonsensical insofar as they imagine that machines will evolve beyond them, as they have evolved beyond orang-utans. Machines could evolve — which is different from being developed — only if they possessed the intelligent will to do so. That they don't possess such a will is proved by their inability to fight back when the vital Erewhonians, who do possess such a will, decide to destroy them for the sake, as it were, of living lives free of the assembly line and the nuclear reactor. The purely material, inorganic aggregate hasn't the privilege of consciousness: that is reserved for the ensouled, organic stuff we call life, even the lowest forms of which, Butler argues, display a capacity for spontaneous decision eternally denied the most sophisticated engine. It is salutary to realize that the human species will be surpassed like any other, but it is a blasphemous fallacy to believe that anything purely material is going to do the surpassing. Only what proceeds from and in the spirit can be said to have life and, by evolving, to seek to have it more abundantly.

That is the ground of dogma upon which the superstructure of Butler's demonstrations rests. The major indictment against the dogma is that he has projected human qualities of will and intelligence downward onto all other forms of life, an act which may be the prerogative of the poet, "beckon[ing] to the dream," but is not the prerogative of the responsible scientist. As we have seen, however, the responsible scientist must project his peculiar dream too: he must lay down a starting assumption — whether, in our context, spirit is a reality in the universe, or not — before he can at all interpret the data which he industriously gathers. It is not my purpose to grapple with the epistemological issue here at stake, but there does seem to be a consensus among philosophers of science that Butler's recall to undemonstrable postulates is inescapable, and that the test among competing postulates lies in measuring the results each yields us — which means, ultimately, the degree to which we can live by it happily.

That brings us back to The Way of All Flesh. The characters who implicitly assume that anyone's survival depends on the luck of the draw, the accidental inheritance of qualities which go with the milieu at hand, will proceed to expect that their own survival depends on the luck of the draw. They will, for example, marry as Christina marries: she puts aside her desire for a Byronic hero and plays cards with her sisters to see who will win the not exactly Byronic son of Cambridge whom chance has brought to help her papa on Sundays.[6] She doesn't even cheat with the cards: she merely, resignedly hopes. As I shall discuss later, this inert non-strategy of just waiting to see what fortuitously will happen seems to receive a sort of endorsement at certain moments in Ernest's career. But in fact such a posture, even if dignified by a phrase like Wordsworth's "wise passivity," could never extricate Ernest from the nets which entangle him. His slightest movement toward a richer life presupposes a desire which does something to achieve it. If he were simply to wait for a lucky break, he would drift; and a lucky break, even if it came, could not forever keep him from drifting onto the rocks. Sooner or later his boat would break up. And if the something which he actively did were, like a good Darwinian creature, to try his strength against his enemies', he would succeed at best in destroying them along with himself, whether the weapon were the penknife or the pound. The something he does must, to the extent that he would come into a richer life at all, be intelligent and vital, purposing among other things to get along better with his enemies, not to exterminate them.

We can appreciate the ambitiousness of Butler's dogma by comparing it not only to Darwin's, with which it has an obvious family resemblance as an evolutionary theory, but to Hume's. Like Hume, Butler wants to find a ground for belief in God which is different from that entertained by the vulgar, who are stirred to speculation about the invisible powers by fear — fear of the vagaries of nature, like floods, thunderstorms, sudden deaths; fear of contrary turns in human affairs, like usurpations, assassinations, robberies; or fear of what comes after death. Belief in God — what Hume calls theism — ought to be grounded in an apprehension of the final causes of nature, in an instinctive "feeling" for its structure and design, whence, in the phrase already quoted, "the idea of a contriver...immediately flow[s] in upon you with a force like that of sensation." By taking the requisite "time, reflection, and study," Hume's mouthpiece Philo does of course "summon up those...objections, which can support infidelity," but however logically interesting, they are practically "frivolous" and "abstruse," "mere cavils and sophisms," when weighted against *the sensation* of "the beauty and fitness of final causes."

> How [Philo asks] could things have been as they are, were there not an original, inherent principle of order somewhere, in thought or in matter? And it is very indifferent to which of these we give the preference. Chance has no place, on any hypothesis, sceptical or religious. Everything is surely governed by steady, inviolable laws.[7]

As we have noted, Hume goes no further than this bare proposition which, for readers who cannot trust Philo, he repeats *in propria persona* at the head of *The Natural History of Religion*: "The whole frame of nature bespeaks an intelligent author; and no rational enquirer can, after serious reflection, suspend his belief a moment with regard to the primary principles of genuine Theism and Religion."[8] From this, Hume believes, we can infer nothing about either human or divine morality. Butler lacks the fear of the skeptical angel. When he "anatomize[s] the eye" or "contemplate[s] the suppleness or variety of joints in his fingers," he discerns evidence not just of design, but of direction. The creature whose eye is so sharp and whose fingers are so manipulable, must have desired to see and to handle more of the world than his forebears did. And those who come after will possess eyes and hands that will be still better, for the effects of desire are cumulative.

Who fashions the way along which all flesh must travel? Who gives direction to the evolution of eyes and hands? Not a deity who creates *ab extra*, like Paley's perdurable watchmaker. Butler rejects both that itinerant, who leaves his product behind to tick-tock on by itself, and the mechanistic metaphor which goes with him. Given an evolving world like ours, the proper metaphor for creation is organic, and the habitation of the creator is *within*, just as Christ said. While the salvationist churchman has objected to Butler's removing God from the altar painting and putting him in the flesh of the living, the Marxist has complained, in Arnold Kettle's words, that his "overall philosophy...is less rigid, more unprincipled, so to speak, than life itself...."[9] For the Marxist, life is "principled" in the sense that it proceeds according to an economic pattern toward a preconceived end. Butler wants no pattern imposed upon life — not, at least, one imposed from the future, which in the rigorous Marxist vein is the ultimate invitation to dictatorship, and which in the merely anxious Tennysonian vein, with its trust in progress toward that "one far-off divine event/To which the whole creation moves" (*In Memoriam*, Epilogue, 143–44), is the ultimate and complementary invitation to quietism.

He is willing enough to admit that a pattern is imposed from the past, to notice, in all common sense, how much of a creature's life is determined by ancestral experience: if we are mammals, we can't all at once return to being fishes. More, in the essay "God the Known and God the Unknown," he fancies that the world itself might be "remembering" how to grow, attentive to the experience of parent worlds preceding it, much as a human embryo remembers its ancestors' lives by putting on the gills of a fish and the tail of a monkey. Thus Clara Stillman is not quite accurate in saying that Butler has no traffic with design from without. But she is perfectly right in saying that, for him, a creature "has no final goal in view...no vision of remote consequences any more than the man who invented the kettle had a vision of the locomotive."[10] Though a creature may be doubly determined from behind — both by the cumulative experience of everything in its line since the *Urschleim*, and by the genetic memory bequeathed by the parents of the world itself — it is free to live toward the future according to its own lights. It is not doomed slavishly to repeat the experience of its predecessors, or to suffer the surprises of spontaneous mutations, and nothing more. However gradually and stumblingly, it can effect something different in itself to meet the discomforts of a new environment or a new competitor.

II

Hume found nothing in the design of the universe to recommend it morally — no evidence of justice or benevolence in the creating or sustaining acts of nature. Rather out of harmony with his usual dispassioned gentleness, the disgust he exhibits would satisfy Sartre:

> How hostile and destructive [creatures are] to each other! How insufficient all of them for their own happiness! How contemptible or odious to the spectator! The whole presents nothing but the idea of a blind nature, impregnated by a great vivifying principle, and pouring forth from her lap, without discernment or parental care, her maimed and abortive children.... The true conclusion is, that the original source of all things is entirely indifferent to all these [moral] principles, and has no more regard to good above ill than to heat above cold, or to drought above moisture, or to light above heavy.

This *contemptus mundi* statement has at least something to do with an anthropocentric ethics which, though perfectly in place in the *Treatise* or the *Inquiry*, where Hume is concerned with human conduct, are a trifle myopic here in the *Dialogues*, where he is concerned with matters that to some degree transcend the merely human. When Philo derides the imperfection and amorality of nature, he expresses the very anthropocentrism for which he has criticized Cleanthes. "Thus," to take but one instance, "the winds are requisite to convey the vapours along the surface of the globe, and to assist men in navigation: But how oft, rising up to tempests and hurricanes, do they become pernicious?"[11]

Butler wouldn't deny that, from the sailor's point of view, a storm is a great evil. But he would urge a rather wider view when the good or evil of the universe is in question. First, he sees benignity at work not simply where organisms are improving their lot — that is easy enough — but throughout the whole creation, for there is always the freedom for organisms at least to try to improve their lot: for men, say, to do what they ingeniously can to weather hurricanes by building stronger ships, or to dodge them by building more effective forecasting instruments. Again, organisms aren't doomed to enact a pattern that has been all worked out beforehand, or to respond willy-nilly to the charming or ugly whims of "a blind nature." Second, Butler believes the triumph of the good to be progressive. Genesis misleads us by saying God was satisfied with his work when he saw it was good. Such a deity has "little hope of...improving. He was satisfied with his own work, and that is fatal."[12] The true God is never satisfied: one can observe him over geological history trying form after form as, in and through the creatures who are his members, he seeks a life that is more gentle, more comely, more at peace than that which has hitherto been tried.

The publication of *The Origin of Species* made it possible for Butler to take seriously the view which Hume playfully insists must follow from the supposition that God is imperfect and finite: "Many worlds might have been botched and bungled, throughout an eternity, ere this system was struck out: Much labour lost: Many fruitless trials made: And a slow, but continued improvement carried on during infinite ages in the art of world-making."[13] Since the world is in fact evolving, the "botched and bungled" versions are not evil in the orthodox sense at all; they are mistakes inevitable in the trying. Some rebels against orthodoxy have supposed the "cruelties of nature" to be the malicious deeds of Nobodaddy; less Manichean rebels have supposed worse — that the cruelties are just the fortuitous events Darwin says they are, and that Nobodaddy is a fiction. But Butler would answer with Shaw that Nobodaddy isn't a fiction: he is an imposter who "could not have impersonated anybody if there had not been Somebodaddy to impersonate" — a Somebodaddy living in and through all things. As Butler writes:

> ...the Theologian dreams of a God sitting above the clouds among the cherubim, who blow their loud uplifted angel trumpets before Him, and humour Him as though He were some despot in an Oriental tale; but we enthrone Him upon

the wings of birds, on the petals of flowers, on the faces of our friends, and upon whatever we most delight in of all that lives upon the earth. We then can not only love Him, but we can do that without which love has neither power nor sweetness, but is a phantom only, an impersonal person, a vain stretching forth of arms towards something that can never fill them — we can express our love and have it expressed to us in return. And this not in the uprearing of stone temples — for the Lord dwelleth in temples made with other organs than hands — nor yet in the cleansing of our hearts, but in the caress bestowed upon horse and dog, and kisses upon the lips of those we love.[14]

Butler is promulgating a religion of progress, whose saints are not just the human beings Comte reverenced, but all the diverse forms of life that have succeeded in making new things possible for them who come after. They found their lives — they were canonized and thus given an extended freehold on existence — by losing them. Not all the saints have been memorialized in art: most indeed are remembered unconsciously, either in the morphology of our bodies — say, in the now more or less inutile tail bone which is retained and worshipped like a holy relic of those early primates who fashioned their tails for the sake of balance — or in the stages of our development — say, the quick year and a half within which infants learn to toddle, a period of thanksgiving to those thousands of generations of man-apes who first married form and content in the art of walking upright. Butler's is also a religion with an unfixed eschatology. Though there is no city of God towards which all things inexorably are tending, there have been and will be *cities* of God which all things build freely as they wish. The past-masterful accomplishments of our generation are, archaeologically speaking, built on top of many cities wherein our ancestors did apprenticeships, and our own present-day apprenticeships will contribute to the glories of future cities. If enough of us were to develop the habit of reading, for example, then it is conceivable that many generations hence babies with richer memories than ours would be no more conscious of learning to read than we are of learning to talk.[15] And the time and effort saved would in turn enable them to respond to the needs which they, in their advanced dissatisfaction, may discern, but which we, in our comparative vulgarity, are blind to.

Though we can perceive a Butlerian hagiography and eschatology along these general lines, we perceive very little conscious worship of the past or prayerful expectation of the future. This is not to say, as Basil Willey does, that the ways of what Butler calls the known God of this world have "no power to inspire reverence or demand service," or that Butler himself has "little or no sense of the holy."[16] Rather, we are being urged to direct our religious emotions to the here and now. However demonstrably continuous we are with all life, past and future, over the millennia of evolutionary time; however continuous we are, more immediately, with the lives of our parents and our children, we ought to reverence and serve ourselves first of all, for if we aren't accommodated we can't reverence and serve anyone. And second, we should reverence and serve those creatures who are separate enough from us not to be competitors — "birds ... flowers ... friends ... horse and dog" — and yet not so separate as to inspire aversion, as certain bacilli, worms, or crustacea might do. True, we are organically continuous even with these, but our instinct shuns any suggestion of "practical" identity. Organically and socially there is richer and more complex continuity between us and our parents or offspring, but again our instinct knows that in practice it is no use. "We want to be ourselves; we do not want any one else to claim part and parcel of our identity. This community of identities is not found to answer in everyday life" (LH, 80).

Theobald understands this as soon as he discovers that the infant Ernest, who is of course all spit, stools, cries and gurgles, is not in the least the replica of himself that he has wanted:

> If Christina could have given birth to a few full-grown clergymen in priest's orders — of moderate views, but inclining rather to Evangelicism, with comfortable livings and in all respects facsimiles of Theobald and Christina themselves — why there might have been more sense in it; or if people could buy ready-made children of whatever age and sex they liked at a shop instead of always having to make them at home and to begin at the beginning with them — that might do better, but as it was he did not like it. (WAF, 78)

Ernest soon comes not to "like it" either, but it takes him a long time to realize what Theobald never realizes: that the best way to come to "like it" is by letting those too-near dear ones be. Neither torment them with anger nor smother them with affection, but approach amity with them in the only way it can be approached — by being in a state of amity with oneself.

This egoism might be opposed by those who piously think children would be more reverent in thinking first of their parents, and parents in thinking first of their children, and all in thinking next of the greater species and ecosystem of which they are parts. Suppose, Butler answers, that I am a blood corpuscle and that, by effort of meditation, I discover I am not only living in my own canal, but am blessedly part of an animal which will continue to live after I am reprocessed, and in which I therefore enjoy eternal life — or what to my poor mind must seem eternal life. The insight will occasion a brief, dull amusement, but will bring me no real advantage. And if I were the animal unlucky enough to contain a mystical blood corpuscle? Why then "I should conceive he served me better by attending to my blood and making himself a successful corpuscle, than by speculating about my nature. He would serve me best by serving himself best, without being over curious. I should expect that my blood might suffer if his brain were to become too active" (*LH*, 90–91).

It doesn't take a moment to realize that this admonition, so akin to a Carlyle's or a Ruskin's call to forget insoluable questions and do the work at hand, is directed against Butler himself. He was a trouble-making mystical unit within the bodies of his family, his Church, and his nation's intellectual establishments, and though constantly noting his continuity with these bodies, he was forever finding himself, by dint of reflection, in a posture of secession — an Ishmael of the house of Abraham. He cannot heed his own dictum that one ought to be more self-interested. He cannot be like Isaac, who, in spite of inconvenient journeys for unstated purposes, makes himself quite comfortable by simply doing the old man's bidding. He cannot, that is to say, put down his speculative, other-oriented urge, puzzling not only beyond the narrow concerns of how he can "mak[e] himself a successful corpuscle," but beyond both the widely satisfying pieties of the popular supernaturalism, which places the kingdom of God in Rome or Canterbury or Boston, and the esoterically satisfying pieties of natural supernaturalism, which places the kingdom upon the face of Mt. Snowdon or in a field of daffodils — wherever, in big or little, the sublime spirit of the knowable God reveals itself. This latter kind of mystical reflection would be bad enough, but Butler does worse: he lets himself brood over the truth of Jesus' remark that the kingdom is not after all of this world: the world's body may have descended from the unknown God(s) of prior worlds, or may be but a corpuscle within a larger universal body, or but an embryo from which another world, with a larger share of godhead, may evolve. Such a series of Brunoesque possibilities — an infinity of worlds within worlds — is as irrelevant as it is fascinating. And more than irrelevant: to brood like this may bring suffering on the "blood" and body to which Butler belongs. That is why he so frequently pulls himself up short by proclaiming the wisdom of egoism, or by temperately observing the futility of trying to "pierce the veil that hides it [the presence of the unknown God] from human eyes," for he can "know [no] more about it than its bare existence." If a man must go in for speculation, let it be in the realm of the known God — let it go no further than the natural supernaturalism which ruminates this side of the veil. Suffice it that he overthrow the anthropomorphism of popular supernaturalism, which personifies the goodness of "justice, hope, wisdom, etc." either in the figures of separate deities or in the figure of a supreme one. Suffice it that he believe "that people [will] no more cease to love God [or these aspects of goodness which are called divine] on ceasing to believe in His objective personality, than they had ceased to love justice on discovering that she was not really personal; nay, that they would never truly love Him till they saw Him thus." And suffice it that, should he desire to "objectify" God, he do so by shunning disputation and turning to worship what is handsome in the things of this world. Higgs speaks for Butler when he says:

> ...I have seen a radiance upon the face of those who were worshipping the divine either in art or nature — in picture or statue — in field or cloud or sea — in man, woman, or child — which I have never seen kindled by any talking about the nature and attributes of God. Mention but the word divinity, and our sense of the divine is clouded.[17]

There is a moderating balance struck in that statement which avoids the extremes of, on the one hand, fantastic absorption in the ineffable qualities of the unknown God, whose "goodness" surely transcends "man's highest conception[s]" of what is good, and on the other hand, dull acquiescence in the superstitions of ordinary people like Arowhena, with whom Higgs is arguing. To keep this balance Butler must play up the weaker of the extreme parties: he must extol under the banner of "grace" the virtues of dull acquiescence, in order to keep in bounds his own energetic fantasticality — the very gift which has given him a philosophical daemon to be moderated. Hence the resignation of saying that "genius was like offences — needs must that it come, but woe unto that man through whom it comes. A man's business...is to think as his neighbours do, for Heaven help him if he thinks good what they count bad" (E, 189; cf. LH, 32). Genius is always offensive because it entails unneighborliness, an unamiable going against the grain. This, plus the patently hard work of delving into the unknown, seeking unheard of solutions to novel predicaments, inevitably takes its toll. The genius suffers the torments of martyrs, like those of the gasping fish who first tried to survive on dry land, or like those of the astronomers who offered men the unwelcome news that the sun was a third-rate star, and earth its satellite. Look in the shop-windows at photographs of eminent men, in whatever branch of science or art, and see what the effort of intellectual labor has wrought upon the faces of "nine out of every ten of them." They traffic in "principles," which are elementary devices "suitable for beginners only...[H]e who has so little mastered them as to have occasion to refer to them consciously, is out of place in the society of well-educated people." Next to the amiable and unintrospective Europeans "who were too busy trying to exist pleasantly to trouble their heads as to whether they existed or no," how foolish Descartes appears with his straw of a Cogito.

> They [the "nice" people] felt the futility of the whole question, and were thankful to one who seemed to clench the matter with a cant catchword, especially with a catchword in a foreign language; but how one, who was so far gone as to recognize that he could not prove his own existence, should be able to comfort himself with such a begging of the question, would seem unintelligible except upon the ground of exhaustion.

The only excuse Descartes can have is identical with the one excuse of all genius — namely his having made more easy the lives of "the most fortunate kind of modern European," by having given them "a cant catchword" to allay any philosophical queasiness that has the impudence to attack them. Thanks to Descartes, those who are leading pleasant and healthy lives need never enter the labyrinths of philosophy, out of which there is no rational thread to follow anyway; like "the best class...of our English youth, who live much in the open air,...[they need], as Lord Beaconsfield finely said, never read." They have as little reason to learn to read as does the Venus of

Milo or the St. George of Donatello, both of whom, had they the need or desire "to study," would have "no lack of brains to do it with." Their brains, and the full burden of knowledge their entire bodies so easily carry, are their inheritance from the many generations of pioneering geniuses, most of them "both ugly and disagreeable," who braved the pain of acquiring consciously the abilities which *they* (the heirs) at last enjoy unconsciously (*LH*, 19–32). Like the valiant and illiterate signers of the Magna Charta, whom Victorian anti-intellectuals like Kingsley or Samuel Smiles never ceased admiring, the heirs have that perfect knowledge which is got, in Bunyan's phrase, "by root of heart."

Because the pioneering genius hasn't got his knowledge by root of heart, he can scarcely enjoy the real benefits of it. He is like Moses insofar as he toils under the rule of law — beginner's principles — and is therefore excluded from the kingdom of grace, though with the vision of a prophet he may glimpse it from Pisgah. In practice, the kingdom of grace is something a person must inherit; like money, it is best when it is "old," when it comes from generations who have learned to deploy it responsibly. In one sense, all of us have had a share of "old" grace. Invidious distinctions between good health and bad, old money and new, any money and none, usually aren't drawn till a person has been thrown into the world. In the beginning all full-term infants, "even the lowest idiot, [or] the most contemptible in health or beauty, may...reflect with pride that they *were born*" (*LH*, 61). The achievements of a Descartes or a Newton, who rarely live past their three score and ten, seem paltry when compared to the quiet achievements of every embryo, who passes through stages summarizing millions of years of life. As Erewhon believes, the unborn, the heirs of all the ages, are the truly contented, flawlessly doing their job, never differing from their parents on all the main questions, such as where the eyes should go, and where the thyroid. And if the best is to be in intrauterine paradise, the next best is to be young. Butler contrives his own version of the Romantic myth of childhood, one the more poignant because so unlike his own:

> It is the young and fair, then, who are the truly old and truly experienced; it is they who alone have a trustworthy memory to guide them; they alone know things as they are, and it is from them that, as we grow older, we must study if we would still cling to truth. The whole charm of youth lies in its advantage over age in respect of experience, and where

this has for some reason failed, or been misapplied, the charm is broken. When we say that we are getting old, we should say rather that we are getting new or young, and are suffering from inexperience, which drives us into doing things which we do not understand, and lands us, eventually, in the utter impotence of death. The kingdom of heaven is the kingdom of little children. (*LH*, 244)

But there are little children and little children. Those who best retain their title to the kingdom are blessed in many ways, but chiefly in coming from "zoösperms who have entered into the kingdom of heaven before [them] for many generations" (*WAF*, 241). That is, they come from forebears who have been bred "in health and beauty," and who therefore have had the gentle temperaments that go along with bodies which need neither spite nor envy anyone, least of all "the young and fair" offspring who are growing up round them.

III

Proud though he may be that he *was born*, Ernest, like any other frail child, must have had intrauterine misgivings about the way his limbs were being formed. And his misgivings mount sharply when he discovers that his parents are not handsome and nice, but just the opposite, and that instead of allowing him to be a child, and thus to pleasure in the "experience" his zoöspermatic heritage has given him, they try to make him a grown-up right away, putting him in positions for which he has no instinct, and which expose his "inexperience." If intrauterine paradise is best, then, as they believe in Erewhon, birth must be a kind of dying. Or, "returning to the common use of words," mightn't we at least wonder, Butler asks, whether there be "any decrepitude so awful as childhood in a happy united God-fearing family?" (*WAF*, 27).

The opening chapters analyze why, in the Pontifex family, being young has changed from something paradisal to something purgatorial. Ernest's great-grandfather must have been a happy child. Growing up in rural England in the eighteenth century was, in Butler's eyes, an enviable experience, and the joy of old Pontifex's youth was extended by the occupations of his adulthood — his facility with charcoal and on the organ, his industry as a carpenter, his kindness to children. His son George breaks with this unintrospective life. He goes to the city, teaches himself the classics, learns the language of English prigs who look at the wrong paintings in the

Uffizi, and, in short, becomes cerebral and insincere about things which to his father had been either uninteresting or unconscious. The primal zoösperm of old Pontifex is the one the zoösperm of Ernest will have to remember if he is to stand a chance of recovering life after the death of birth. Meanwhile, George's son Theobald inherits hardly anything to help him cope with the urban environment his father's new brains and new money have taken by storm: "the more brilliant the success in any one generation, the greater as a general rule the subsequent exhaustion until time has been allowed for recovery" (WAF, 19). Fortunately, Theobald's exhaustion does not indicate permanent amnesia within the family. His sister Alethaea is her grandfather's favorite, and she keeps the zoöspermatic tradition alive, not through her womb, of course, but through her spirit, her broker, and her attorney. First she stimulates her young godson's "memory" for healthy activities — building organs, playing Handel, and copying the manners of nice boys — and second she bequeaths him the worldly sign of good forebears, an abundance of the well-husbanded and as it were congealed zoösperm, pounds sterling. She does more than anyone to push him off the starting-blocks in his particular "race for unconsciousness" (LH, 30).[18]

If getting off the starting-blocks called mainly for cunning, Ernest would still be there. But like most people who don't die in infancy, he need have little to do with cunning; he has just enough of what Erewhon (but not Butler altogether) regards as the one thing needful: "the only fit object of human veneration," good luck (E, 113). It bestows not simply the health and savvy engendered by desirable forebears, but the money which health and savvy usually manage to pile up. Ernest's passivity thus puts on the robe — the bathrobe — of virtue. By being lazy at school he attains mediocrity, eluding both the priggishness of scholarly excellence and the unsightliness of social rebellion, extremes which would demand committed effort. By staying alive for twenty-seven years he comes into his money. By just waiting around he lets evaporate the curacy, family, and associates he has not had the pluck to sweep away: "He should not have had the courage to give up all for Christ's sake, but now Christ [again, his own will to happiness which in effect tells him just to wait around] had mercifully taken all; and lo! it seemed as though all were found" (WAF, 260). Waiting, laughing, loafing, letting taste and events clear away the humbug: virtue rests not in arduous obedience to Theobald, who is cordial only toward Latin, Greek, dowdy women, and the Thirty-nine Articles, but in passive obedience to the "Ernest that dwelt within," who speaks to him at school in stout Elohist language:

> This conscious self of yours, Ernest, is a prig — begotten of prigs, and trained in priggishness; I will not allow it to shape your actions, though it will doubtless shape your words for many a year to come.... Obey me, your true self, and things will go tolerably well with you, but only listen to that outward and visible old husk of yours which is called your father, and I will rend you in pieces unto the third and fourth generation as one who has hated God; for I, Ernest, am the God who made you. (WAF, 116)

Of course even passive obedience must do things. So Ernest rebelliously sells a dull Sallust or dictionary in order to buy "those cheap editions of the great [Handel] oratorios," and he steals time from lessons in order to play the organ in St. Michael's, to look at a window designed by Dürer, or to talk to the old rector who knew Dr. Burney, who in turn had broken bounds as a schoolboy at Chester "that he might watch Handel smoking his pipe in the Exchange coffee house" — thus bringing himself "in[to] the presence of one who, if he had not seen Handel himself, had at least seen those who had seen him" (WAF, 140). These details are not trivial, for they are signs of Ernest's learning to move among the primary and associative pleasures of eye and ear, and, "though he dared not openly avow it," to feel right about disobeying his father (WAF, 139).

Ernest's good luck comes in two interdependent forms. One is biological: he inherits his great-grandfather's capacity to appreciate Handel's music or Dürer's windows. The other form is (loosely) circumstantial: there just happen to be at St. Michael's a friendly organist and rector to encourage the development of his inherited capacity into an ability. Sometimes Ernest's circumstantial luck works in the crude but not altogether incredible mode of direct intervention, as when John the coachman cows Theobald into "leav[ing] Master Ernest...to the reproaches of his own conscience" instead of beating him for having helped Ellen, or when the same John turns up again years later to rescue Ernest from the consequences of having married her. Circumstantial luck works in a subtler and more easily credible mode, however, when the remarks or just the carriage of people casually met stirs up a dormant feeling in Ernest and sends him in a new direction. We have already looked at the kindly negative which Mr. Shaw the tinker gives to Ernest's assumptions about the historicity of the resurrection. Similarly, Ernest is embarrassed by the vacuity of his missionary "call" when, having mounted the stairs to convert the quiet Methodist couple, he realizes he doesn't at all know what he is supposed to convert them *from*. But most compelling are the three decided *No*'s which Towneley returns to his "Don't you like poor people very much yourself?", and which register on his unconscious the plain fact "that no one was nicer for being poor," and the strong possibility that one might well be nicer *a*) for being rich, and *b*) for "trying to get on comfortably in the world" instead of "trying to lead a quiet unobtrusive life of self-devotion" (*WAF*, 221–22).

Getting rich is largely a function of circumstantial luck: either there is somebody ready to leave money to Ernest, or there isn't. But learning how to get on comfortably, "and to look, and be, as nice as possible," is more a function of biological luck — of Ernest's having inherited not only the instincts for enjoyment and gentleness, but the aptitude for culling and assimilating those good instincts out of the mess of bad ones — the tendencies to earnestness, priggishness, ethereality — which he has also inherited. He must display this aptitude as, so to speak, he reviews the zoöspermatic lineage, the organic givens, which he can choose either to cultivate or to suppress. Here, quite obviously, passivity is not enough: Ernest must do the work of discrimination. There have been times when a young man could uncritically assimilate *all* of his parents' qualities, as, according to Herodotus, an Asian tribesman would actually eat his deceased parents, in recognition of the fact that they were what he *was* in the material sense, and were what he *wanted to be* in the spiritual (*LH*, 114). Ernest can't immediately alter the material substance his parents gave him, but he can strive to suppress the spiritual substance they gave, and to reject that which they attempt to foster. He must decline the spiritual food labelled Theobald and Christina. When the dish labelled Grandpa George comes round, though, he may safely nibble. For the man lived long and comfortably, and in spite of his preferring Raphael to Giotto and of his writing Childe Haroldish drivel opposite Mont Blanc, he had a vague instinct for the *right* way of all flesh — to wit, "that the principal business of life is to enjoy it," as "All animals, except man, know" perfectly well (*WAF*, 73). Yet Ernest's chief diet must be his great-grandfather, who not only lived long and comfortably, but had a sharp instinct for the right way just referred to, and followed it with much undeliberate good humor. His is the posture Ernest assumes on the day he leaves Roughborough, quietly gazing at the setting sun and talking to it, till in unsentimental gold it shines forth a promise of contentment and money:

> Was it to be always sin, shame and sorrow in the future, as it had been in the past, and the ever-watching eye and protecting hand of his father laying burdens on him greater than he could bear — or was he too some day or another to come to feel that he was fairly well and happy?... Still looking into the eye of the sun and smiling dreamily, he thought how he had helped to burn his father in effigy, and his look grew merrier till at last he broke out into a laugh — exactly at this moment the light veil of cloud parted from the sun, and he was brought back to terra firma by the breaking forth of the sunshine. (WAF, 171)

The old man's comic sense, his carpentry, his taste for music, his empathy for children — all these traits are potential in Ernest, waiting to be brought forth by lucky circumstance and by his own receptivity and exertion. When the sun rains down on him and he gets his £70,000, he is endowed with the means which ought to help him raise these traits to a very high power. One may well wish to quarrel with his way of using that means, as I shall discuss later. But one is at least inclined to let him pleasure in his good circumstantial luck in his own way, because one sees how, compared with the luckiest, his biological luck — that which the £70,000 is supposed to embellish — is only so-so. That, at any rate, is how it seems to him, and indeed if a man considers himself somehow unfortunate, then he is — if only because his discouragement keeps him from using what he has to the utmost.

Ernest's grey Ulster suit is like Towneley's, but his limbs do not fill it as Towneley's would. Back in intrauterine paradise Towneley's limbs were shaping themselves to wear grey Ulster with inimitable grace, while Ernest's were dooming themselves to awkwardness, so that "At thirteen or fourteen he was a mere bag of bones, with upper arms about as thick as the wrists of other boys of his age..." (WAF, 113). Who cares how natty Towneley is, or how shabby Ernest? One can have no interest in defending Butler's particular choice for an anti-self — "[his] notion of everything [he] should most like to be" (WAF, 314) — especially when one knows the lineaments of the character of Towneley's original, Charles Paine Pauli.[19] One could attribute Butler's reverence for Towneley to the mood of hero worship general throughout the nineteenth century, from Scott and Carlyle to Tennyson and Yeats. It represented a vitalizing antidote to the age's intellectual anxieties and emotional ennui, as well as a pastel-toned escape from its crowded ugliness. But I think it worthwhile to defend the always useful psychological strategy of defining an anti-self which, though an image of what, in Yeats's phrase, one has "handled least, least looked upon," is nevertheless visible, near at hand, and of one's own species, and can therefore inspire service and emulation rather than despair and abasement. My case is similar to Hume's, in his praise of the easy irrationality of polytheism over the intense rationality of monotheism. It is no doubt correct, he says, to think of the one high God — God the unknown — as infinitely distant and superior. But before God the mind sinks into the lowest submission, and tends "to represent the monkish virtues of mortification, penance, humility, and passive suffering, as the only qualities which are acceptable to him." When man thinks of the gods as, on the other hand, but a little above him, as beings whose ancestors may once have been mortal like himself, he may "without profaneness" look to rival or emulate them. "Hence," Hume writes, "activity, spirit, courage, magnanimity, love of liberty, and all the virtues which aggrandize a people."[20] Ernest's worship of Towneley is, *pro tempore*, an advance upon his worship of the Jehovah for whom his father was vicar, for though he continues to abase himself — "The people like Towneley are the only ones who know anything that is worth knowing, and like that of course I can never be" (*WAF*, 286–87) — he yet is stimulated to emulation. It is in a very small way, naturally: he lays out his money on Towneleyesque grey Ulster, a lavish portmanteau, trips to the Continent, and so on. Pathetic, yes, but nevertheless a beginning, empowered by the reasonable hope that his heirs may emulate Towneley in the larger ways of being as insouciant, as handsome, as virile; and may even surpass him by harmonizing these achievements of the body with those of the mind — those which Ernest currently deprecates as the mere hewing of wood and drawing of water that "make[s] Towneleys possible," but which surely can lay the foundations for a "grace" any Towneley would bow before.

So Ernest's attitude is in principle a proper balance between an active emulation of what his time offers as "the most fortunate kind of modern European," and a quiet acceptance of himself as he is. And if my analysis is correct, his self-acceptance is the basis for his hope successfully to rival "the most fortunate," and so glean an immortality they shall not have. This is a theme I shall turn to in my final chapter, but at present I want to add one more note in justification of Butler's tolerance for Ernest at the end of the novel. It has to do with his tolerance for himself, to be sure, but also with his tolerance for his progenitors.

IV

Unless one is a thorough Erewhonian, which Butler isn't, one doesn't blame people for their bad luck. Of course Butler's resentment is heavy against the parents who conceived him from awkward sperm and ovum, and who ambushed him with stupidities when he was least able to resist, but he recognizes too that they brewed the best juices they had, and that they acted always on the firmest foundation possible, the conventions of their neighbors. Their juices and conventions happen to be bad, but, with an eye on the calendar, tolerate them one must:

> ...it was the system, rather than the people, that was at fault.... As it was, the case was hopeless; it would be no use their even entering into their mothers' wombs and being born again.... The only thing to do with them was to humour them, and to make the best of them till they died — and be thankful when they did so. (*WAF*, 240)

The grudging impatience of that remark doesn't suggest a very sweet tolerance, but Butler shows other signs of tolerance which are a good deal gentler, and which complicate his attitude in a way nobody to my knowledge has noticed. There are his hopeful suppositions as to what the characters of Theobald and Christina would have been under luckier circumstances. She is at bottom "a good-tempered kindly-natured girl...who if she had married a sensible layman — we will say a hotel keeper — would have developed into a good landlady and been deservedly popular with her guests" (*WAF*, 48–49). Theobald too is out of his right milieu. He obscurely knows that "life would be pleasanter if there were no sick sinners [to have to comfort], or if they would at any rate face an eternity of torture with more indifference" (*WAF*, 60). If he could be "in his element," as the farmers, "full-bodied, healthy and contented," are in theirs, he would be a sailor, as he had wanted to when he was a boy. It is as though Ernest's son, so lacking in literary ability and so full of common sense, humor, and practical judgment, were born to live the life Theobald ought to have lived (WAF, 349). Butler is not indulging in petty revenge when he wishes Christina and Theobald had led sub-middle-class lives. The conventions of the middle class have desiccated them, and Butler is simply wishing to put them in the water where they belong. Surely, too, the last third of the novel reveals a general softening toward Christina and Theobald which is not just a function of its being written more than ten years after the first two-thirds, but is also a consequence of the "wrong milieu" premise established at the start. Admittedly though, one can define attitudes toward parents only in relative terms. When talking about a book which contains so much bitter resentment, to say there is a "general softening" means there is a mixing of occasional forgiveness with durable anger.

That explains the divided treatment of Christina's death. Butler-Overton continues to laugh at her fanatical day-dreams about how Ernest should spend his money to make his brother Joey Archbishop of Canterbury, to give Charlotte huge presents every year, and to buy his own way into Parliament where he might become Lord Battersby, etc. (WAF, 325). Butler-Ernest, by contrast, humors her fantasies, allays her fears of hell, and weeps at her bedside:

> "Mother," he said, "forgive me — the fault was mine, I ought not to have been so hard; I was wrong, very wrong." The poor blubbering fellow meant what he said, and his heart yearned to his mother as he had never thought that it could yearn again. (WAF, 322)

The treatment of Theobald is similarly divided. He is still pathetic, as he stands in the living room under the Elijah picture and whistles his two tunes, "In My Cottage Near a Wood" and the Easter hymn, "as a clever bullfinch might whistle them — he had got them but he had not got them right" (WAF, 327). He is still mean, as he prays over Christina, who, doubtful of her election, considers his professional reputation to depend on her at least getting a pass: "'But Christina, they [your sins] are forgiven you'; and then he entrenched himself in a firm but dignified manner behind the Lord's prayer" (WAF, 329). But for the most part the latter-day Theobald is seen as a harmless, pitiable old man, whose final letter is neither hateful nor peevish:

> I keep wonderfully well and am able to walk my five or six
> miles with comfort, but at my age there's no knowing how
> long it will last and time flies quickly. I have been busy
> potting plants all the morning, but this afternoon it is wet.
> (*WAF*, 350)

This passage is followed by placid, commonplace animadversions
on Gladstone's Irish policy and on Charlotte's virtues once as a
daughter and now as a married woman. As for all the ways this man
has let and hindered Ernest, Butler dismisses the pain and incom-
patibility as

> a very common case and a very natural one ... the main
> ground of complaint [lying] in the fact that he [Ernest] had
> become so independent and so rich while still very young,
> and that thus the old gentleman had been robbed of his
> power to tease and scratch in the way which he felt he was
> entitled to do. ... I suppose it is so with all of us. At any rate I
> am sure that most fathers, especially if they are clergymen,
> are like Theobald. (*WAF*, 351)

The sociological indulgence and the personal vendetta — that "tease
and scratch" are a nasty pair of words — co-exist to the end. It is
enough if we remember that the latter doesn't eclipse the former.

3

The Hedonics

We have noted the relevance to Butler of Bacon's epigram: "...a little philosophy inclineth man's mind to atheism; but depth in philosophy bringeth men's minds about to religion."[1] We may say as well that a little philosophy drew Butler into a decadent and complacent kind of hedonism; but depth in philosophy led him into a hedonism which is eminently defensible. Because he ultimately wanted a variously and richly *human* pleasure not only for himself, but for all who desire to have life more abundantly, his moral principles can be said to satisfy Kant's high criterion of universalizability.

We won't appreciate the attractiveness of Butler's ethics, however, if like the Muggeridgean reader we dwell on the few pathetic ways he tried "to pleasure" as he sometimes supposed he ought. The Muggeridgean cannot get over Butler's subconscious homoeroticism and general sexual ineptitude: his lugubrious servility to Pauli, his cowardice before Miss E. M. A. Savage and the lovely daughter of his hotel keeper in Italy, and, most sadly, his addiction to visiting his French prostitute, Lucie Dumas, every Wednesday. This practice, which he infamously justified by the quip that it is cheaper to buy milk than to keep a cow, was made doubly bizarre by his paying Henry Festing Jones's one-pound entry fee to the same Mlle. Dumas every Tuesday, thus managing to mix his seed with his friend's without having to get into bed with him. In sum, he tried to quiet, but no doubt only intensified his loathing of his own sexuality by arranging a once-a-week service to discharge himself, by laying out money to keep off threats of genuine attachment, and, when that failed, by simply running away. This picture of trembling lubricity hardly does Butler justice. As Shaw wrote upon the publication of

Jones's *Memoir*, the weekly pilgrimages to Mlle. Dumas were "obviously a relic of that shallow Hedonism which seemed to the mid-century Victorians to follow logically when they discovered that the book of Genesis is not a scientific account of the origin of species ... [Butler's] mind was too powerful to be imposed on in that way for long. ..."[2] Though he never redeemed his sexual laches, his mind was, as early as *Erewhon*, advancing beyond the "shallow Hedonism" which the new knowledge about the evolution of species seemed to entail.

I

One needs to be very cautious in declaring anything about the locus of meaning in *Erewhon*: Butler's intentions are often difficult to ascertain in the play between Erewhonian documents and spokesmen, and Higgs's naive suppositions and frequently sensible self-doubts. Nevertheless, one can discern how Butler started with the Darwinian equations between fortune and virtue, misfortune and vice, and how, finding that they issued in a crude, egoistic hedonism, he proceeded, by implication, to condemn them.[3] The history of evolution indeed demonstrates that the blessed are those who have luck, and the damned are those who don't. Erewhon therefore seems to be following the laws of nature when it treats physical illness punitively. Since a man is comprised mostly of muscle, bone, and vital organs, if something is wrong with his brain, if he has aberrant ideas tending, say, to fraud or embezzlement, it is a minor matter to be treated medically, for the brain is a small and only recently matured part of his make-up. He has fair chances of surviving an urge to embezzle: he is after all only trying to steal a march on his neighbors in the struggle for existence. But he has almost no chance of surviving tuberculosis: not only can he not keep up with the others' march, but he is a drag upon them.[4]

Now, most readers will approve of one aspect of Erewhonian jurisprudence which had a special pertinence to nineteenth-century England, though it may have had too full a development in our time: namely, the more tolerant treatment of those who commit what we ordinarily call crimes, particularly crimes affecting property. But what about the treatment of the man who is imprisoned for "the great crime of labouring under pulmonary consumption," the why or whence of which is considered irrelevant?

There is no question [says the judge] of how you came to be

wicked, but only this — namely, are you wicked or not?... You tell me that you had no hand in your parentage and education, and that it is therefore unjust to lay these things to your charge.... You may say that it is your misfortune to be criminal; I answer that it is your crime to be unfortunate. (*E*, 115–17)

This may please somebody like H. L. Mencken, who objected to medical expense on the grounds that nature means for sick people to die.[5] And I wouldn't deny that it pleased a certain side of Butler, who loathed his own youthful lack of robustness (which New Zealand more or less remedied), and who was more generally pleased to strike a blow against ascetic Christianity's morbid reverence for the afflicted. But the response of most readers, and surely of most sides of Butler himself, which were free of the *poseur's* belief in the practicability of eugenics, is that the Erewhonian definition of criminality is as wicked as it is logical. To stay one's hand from the consumptive, to try indeed to cure him, may be illogical if one is engaged in the struggle for existence, but that is no obstacle. A policy's illogicality is often one of its chief recommendations: "...extremes are alone logical [Butler writes elsewhere], and they are always absurd, the mean is alone practicable and it is always illogical" (*WAF*, 265). If Paul was willing to be a fool for Christ, to go against the common sense of the race by saying he would gain his life by losing it — then Butler was willing, *in propria persona*, to be a fool for the consumptive.

Next, I think most readers are repulsed by the shallow, life-denying Erewhonian attitudes toward pregnancy and old age. They are practicably inconsistent about the pregnant woman, for though their strictest ethicists condemn her for being "out of health that good may come," most Erewhonians accept her as a biological necessity, "passing over [her condition] in silence." About old age, however, they are absurdly consistent:

...people had become so clever at dissembling — they painted their faces with such consummate skill — they repaired the decay of time and the effects of mischance with such profound dissimulation...[that] marriages were often contracted with most deplorable results, owing to the art with which infirmity had been concealed. (*E*, 136)

It is not enough to rejoin that the Erewhonian mistake is in having missed the Samaritan's satisfaction in curing the sick, or the woman's exhilaration in bringing forth a child, or the beauty of old age — the ripeness and stillness attained, as D. H. Lawrence says in a poem, when "people [live] without accepting lies." One must also rejoin, with the mature Butler himself, that life is not finally to be measured by quantitative rule, that though a sound constitution is of paramount importance, it is never enough. Events like pregnancy and aging ought to be seen not simply in terms of parasitism and degeneration, respectively, but in terms of life's contriving to create and destroy itself, with a recklessness justified by its own vast store. Health is not to be defined merely by blood pressure and muscle tone, but by the mind's activity. What does a man whose chest is clear and whose years are many *do* with his good fortune? We must, for answer, turn from the Erewhonians to someone like John Pontifex, who uses his hale eighty years to build and play upon organs, to draw pictures with a facility that would credit "some good early master," to be kindly to children, and to discourse with the sun. Or to someone like Overton, also living into hale old age, giving himself to his books, his friends, his aesthetic enjoyments. His art (burlesque) may not be of a high order, but he sees the need for spiritual diversion — to use no nobler phrase — which the beautiful but bovine Erewhonians are completely blank about.

II

The nature of Butler's hedonism has been misunderstood because the Erewhonian definition of virtue as physical health and beauty, quantities of money and sensual pleasure, etc., has been taken to be his last word when it is barely his first. David Grylls, for instance, cites what he thinks are contradictions between Butler's postulate that "right is what gives pleasure" and his own small capacity for sensual enjoyment, or between his insistence on the primacy of self-interest and his heroine Alethaea's devoting herself to Ernest.[6] One can discover contradictions here only by assuming that Butler's hedonism is identical with the sensationalistic egoism of someone like Hobbes. The assumption is that everything going by the name of hedonism is reducible to the lowest kind — a misapprehension, and a fear, which we can trace back to Plato.

In the *Philebus*, Socrates supposes — without contestation, of course — that the hedonist will be most supremely happy leading the life of an oyster (1097–98) or an ox (1150); this in turn supposes

that the hedonist is interested only in "impure" pleasures, which are
"movements" of the body within the realm of becoming — i.e., the
realm of animal activities like eating, drinking, and copulating, the
latter giving a pleasure so impure and shameful that it is left to the
dark of night (1148). Socrates allows only the "pure" pleasures of
aesthetic contemplation, which turns from the flecked realm of
becoming to rest its gaze on the unmoving forms of the realm of
being. As a nominalist, Butler disqualifies the Platonic distinction
between being and becoming: the former doesn't exist in Plato's
sense, there are no "fixed forms," because all is changing, and in
directions which aren't predetermined *ab extra.* Pure and impure
pleasures, if those adjectives do indeed suggest the right kind of
distinction, alike occur within the only realm there is — the evolutionary realm of becoming.[7] The pleasure-seeking individual, Butler
maintains, will in fact tend to practice the temperance which Plato
so anxiously adjures us to; but he will do so not because he fears, like
Plato, that if he gives his appetites an ell they will take a mile, and so
cause him to forget intellectual things altogether. He practices
temperance because he has learned that excessive indulgence, like
excessive abstinence, leads to poor health, and so sours his taste for
sensual, as it destroys his capacity for intellectual things.

Butler's emphasis isn't original, of course. Aristotle did something
toward making hedonism respectable, if he did nothing toward
making our terminology more precise, when he said that

> ...the highest good is some sort of pleasure, despite the fact
> that most pleasures are bad and, if you like, bad in the
> unqualified sense of the word. It is for this reason that
> everyone thinks that the happy life is a pleasant life, and
> links pleasure with happiness. And it makes good sense this
> way: for no activity is complete and perfect as long as it is
> obstructed, and happiness is a complete and perfect thing.
> This is why a happy man also needs the goods of the body,
> external goods, and the goods of fortune, in order not to be
> obstructed by their absence.[8]

And like Aristotle, Epicurus insisted that an individual's pleasant
unobstructed activity, whether sensual or intellectual, is possible
only when *prudence* governs his appetites — his intellectual appetites (Butler would add) no less than his sensual. Epicurus' own
emphasis is on the governance of the latter:

> When we say that pleasure is the end, we do not mean the pleasure of the profligate or that which depends on physical enjoyment — as some think who do not understand our teachings...but by pleasure we mean the state wherein the body is free from pain and the mind from anxiety. Neither continual drinking and dancing, nor sexual love, nor the enjoyment of fish and whatever else the luxurious table offers brings about the pleasant life; rather, it is produced by the reason which is sober, which examines the motive for every choice and rejection, and which drives away all those opinions through which the greatest tumult lays hold of the mind.[9]

Though there is more danger of denying the body in Epicurus than in Aristotle, it is significant that, according to Diogenes Laërtius, he adduced "as proof that pleasure is the end...the fact that living things, as soon as they are born, are well content with pleasure and are at enmity with pain, by the prompting of nature and apart from reason."[10] This echoes Aristotle's observation that "the fact that all beasts and all men pursue pleasure is some indication that it is, in a sense, the highest good."[11]

Butler is therefore only being more thorough in gathering evidence when, marvelling at the way the chicken embryo so knowledgeably goes about its business, he explains that it is "attempting to better itself, doing (as Aristotle says all creatures do all things upon all occasions) what it considers most for its advantage under the existing circumstances" (*LH*, 53). The next step is from the indicative ("all creatures *do*") to the imperative ("all creatures *ought*"), a step whose logical difficulties don't trouble Butler a bit, since 1) the difficulties don't seem to have troubled Aristotle, and 2) we have no sure way of judging the claims of one "duty" that is contrary to pleasure, against another. Thus the declaration:

> All animals, except man, know that the principal business of life is to enjoy it — and they do enjoy it as much as man, and other circumstances, will allow. He has spent his life best who has enjoyed it most — God will take care that we do not enjoy it at all more than is good for us. (*WAF,* 73)

This agrees with Aristotle and Epicurus not simply in affirming that pleasure is the end of life, but in cautioning that prudence is the guide toward that end. For Butler means by "God" the intelligence which resides in every organism, and which will "take care" that the organism will find the pleasures most useful and agreeable to it. "The world has long ago settled that morality and virtue are what bring men peace at the last" (WAF, 74). There may be disagreement about which activities lead to peace. Does drinking? How much? Does unkindness to children? How much? Such questions can be answered better by referring to our concrete feelings of pleasure than by referring to some abstract obligation: "When men burn their fingers through following after pleasure they find out their mistake and get to see where they have gone wrong more easily than when they have burnt them through following after a fancied duty, or a fancied idea concerning right virtue" (WAF, 76). So if we take the question of drinking, we see the way Ernest learns how much alcohol is good for him:

> Some of the less desirable boys [at school] used to go to public houses and drink more beer than was good for them; Ernest's inner self can hardly have told him to ally himself to these young gentlemen, but he did so at an early age, and was sometimes made pitiably sick by an amount of beer which would have produced no effect upon a stronger boy; Ernest's inner self must have interposed at this point and told him that there was not much fun in this, for he dropped the habit ere it had taken firm hold over him, and never resumed it.... (WAF, 116)

Or if we take the question of unkindness to children, we see how a shrewder Theobald might notice the point at which making his "children's lives a burden to them" begins to be a burden to him (WAF, 74).

To note the affinities between Butler's ethical theory and that of Aristotle and Epicurus, however, will not exculpate him from the charge of being a narrow egoist — a sort of aesthetical, unpolitical Hobbist. The best way to do him justice is to see him within the tradition of English hedonism, which begins with Hobbes, no doubt, but which finds its most characteristic expression in Hume, who sired the main features of the hedonic utilitarianism systematized by Bentham and humanized by the younger Mill. There is the source of Butlerian ethics — a source the more fruitful because, like his knowledge of digestion, it is preserved in "unconscious memory."[12]

Hume admits Hobbes's contention that ethics are grounded in the self, and for two reasons. First, the moral quality of good or evil resides not in the object or act itself, but in the sensibility of the person who beholds the object or act. The objective relations are the same between a son who kills his father, and a sapling elm which supplants its parent, yet we call the one murder and the other nature.

> The vice entirely escapes you [Hume writes], as long as you consider the object. You never can find it, till you turn your reflexion into your own breast, and find a sentiment of disapprobation, which arises in you, towards this action.... Vice and virtue, therefore, may be compar'd to sounds, colours, heat and cold, which, according to modern philosophy, are not qualities in objects, but perceptions in the mind: And this discovery in morals, like that other in physics, is to be regarded as a considerable advancement of the speculative sciences; tho', like that too, it has little or no influence on practice.[13]

Second, since the feelings of approbation and disapprobation, pleasure and uneasiness, arise in the "breast" of the judging agent, moral statements must at least begin with reference to the self. So, with regard to the marks of "our *natural temper* ... we may justly esteem our *selfishness* to be the most considerable"; and it follows that "There are few occasions when this question 'What is it to me?' is not pertinent."[14] Even the principles of justice derive from self-interest. Men are always more or less selfish because material goods are always more or less scarce. One method of obtaining them is by violence, but "the least reflexion" shows how insecure and hazardous that method is. Instead, men can best satisfy their passion for possessions by establishing the conventions of property, whereby "everyone knows what he may safely possess," and further acquire. The passion for possessions restrains itself for its own interest, knowing "that in preserving society [through observance of the conventions of property], we make much greater advances in the acquiring [of] possessions, than in the solitary and forlorn condition, which must follow upon violence and an universal licence." Hume goes on to describe how the institution of property leads to the institution of justice, based on fulfillment of contractual promises, the doing of services "with a view to some reciprocal advantage," and so on. But I have perhaps said enough to indicate his common ground with Hobbes, in order now to notice his differences with him.

"[C]ertain philosophers [may] delight" in portraying our natural selfishness as though we were "monsters...in fables and romances," but Hume doesn't share their opinion: "...tho' it be rare to meet with one, who loves any single person better than himself; yet 'tis as rare to meet with one, in whom all the kind affections, taken together, do not over-balance all the selfish." Self-interest may be the original motive behind the institution of justice, "but a sympathy with public interest is the source of the moral approbation, which attends that virtue."[15] The key word is "sympathy": that is the Euclidean postulate underlying everything that is non-Hobbist in Hume's ethics, without which he couldn't offer his famous definition of virtue or "personal merit" as "the possession of mental qualities, useful or agreeable to the person himself or to others," with decent emphasis on the last three words. Sympathy is not an arbitrary postulate: Hume draws on many examples from history and from personal experience to give an empirical basis for his belief in the universal existence of a sympathetic human nature. He also shows how our everyday use of general evaluative language presupposes the capacity for disinterested moral judgment. Yet as Butler would point out, he cannot keep men from denying the existence of that capacity. He can only call them fools for doing so, or more effectively, can declare them outside common human nature, as Diogenes and Pascal with their "artificial lives," or the schoolmen with their abstract moral rules, were outside; and appeal instead to "the rest of mankind," who "in every intercourse of business or pleasure, in every discourse and conversation, we shall find ... nowhere ... at any loss upon this subject." The typical phrases in which Hume asserts the existence of sympathy — "How, indeed, can we suppose it possible in anyone who wears a human heart that ...."; "Let us suppose a person ever so selfish ... he must unavoidably feel some propensity to the good of mankind ...."; "... our natural philanthropy ..." — these phrases reveal that for him it is a matter of faith, though, again, of faith which he gives reasons for. The innate ideas of medieval realism, which Locke had presumably banished from philosophy, evidently have to be re-admitted. Hume finds himself unable to "do" ethics without beginning with an inborn capacity for sympathy — for feeling approbation or disapprobation with regard to someone else's case. Moral sympathy must be trained, just as aesthetic sympathy must be, but it is no less a given quality, an "internal sense or feeling which nature has made universal in the whole species."[16]

III

After Butler had read *The Origin of Species*, it was inevitable that he should treat ethics empirically, seeking norms derived not from abstract contemplation, but from direct observation of the facts of experience. Ethics would be for him what they had been for Hume, as much a branch of natural philosophy as physics is. Hume had said that the ethicist only articulates what common-sense people, who have given up their grosser superstitions, have been thinking all along, but, he had added, the articulation is necessary because the schoolmen, in "their passion for hypotheses and systems," have lost touch with common sense.[17] *The Way of All Flesh* is likewise, in its moral argument, a task in the recovery of common sense — "conclusion[s] which sensible people reach without bothering their brains so much" — a task necessary because Butler-Ernest was "not born sensible" (*WAF*, 286). He must "learn laboriously" the foundations of morals by careful observation of how virtuous, thriving people actually behave. Like Hume, he finds 1) that they behave with a high respect for their own material interest, and 2) that they also exhibit a sympathy for others. Let us begin with the first article of common sense.

Observation reveals that the rigors of self-denial which Christianity is supposed to inculcate in its worshippers and its priests are not in fact practiced by most of them. Christians are rather like everybody else, interested more in the full board of Luther and the architecture of Bernini than in the fasts of St. Anthony and the cave of St. Jerome. Those martyrs who died by fire and sword under the Romans were "wrong": their getting killed proved it.[18] The Church survived precisely because there were many who didn't want to die by fire and sword, and they were "right" to the degree that the early Christian communities unself-consciously flourished. Though in their sillier moments Theobald and especially Christina dream about the reputed advantages of martyrdom, they are more truly descendants of those Christians who preferred the immediate goods of life above the coliseum floor. When, in the difficult confinement which she doesn't expect to survive, Christina takes up her pen, she expresses some anxiety about the eternal welfare of her sons, but even more anxiety about the temporal welfare of her husband. All the virtues she exhorts them to — obedience, affection, attentiveness, self-denial, etc. — are highly convenient to parents, who are naturally concerned "lest the offspring should come to have wishes and feelings of its own, which may occasion money difficulties, fancied or real." Perhaps she is fervid for Theobald's earthly well-being, Butler imagines, because she has "a dim unconscious perception" that his heavenly well-being depends on it: "...those who are happy in this world are better and more loveable people than those who are not, and...thus in the event of a resurrection and day of judgment, they will be the most likely to be deemed worthy of a heavenly mansion" (*WAF*, 95). Her primary allegiance is to her husband, and her unconscious self dictates what will be best for him. Her secondary allegiance is to her sons, and her conscious self has an official theory to justify their present sufferings: self-mortification is *their* ticket to heaven, as self-aggrandisement is Theobald's. This sort of double-think works very neatly, for it not only clears the parents' conscience of the charge of having worked against the children's ultimate interests, but provides as well for all their own interests, ultimate and immediate both.

> This was how it came to pass that the children were white and puny. They were suffering from *homesickness*. They were starving through being over-crammed with the wrong things. Nature came down upon them, but she did not come down on Theobald and Christina. Why should she? They were not leading a starved existence. There are two classes of people in this world, those who sin and those who are sinned against; if a man must belong to either he had better do so to the first than to the second. (*WAF*, 97)

If it is better to sin than to be sinned against, or if, indeed, "sin" is a misnomer for the natural pursuit of one's own worldly happiness, then, Butler says, let us drop the hypocrisy which pretends otherwise. The hypocrisy is the more deadly in Theobald and Christina's case because, being undeliberate, it tricks them into behavior that is genuinely sinful: once they have starved their children beyond a certain point, nature really *does* come down on them. They would obviously do better to realize that within the family their interests and the children's are inter-related. Butler's rule is that "A man should not only have his own way as far as possible, but he should only consort with things that are getting their own way so far that they are at any rate comfortable" (*WAF*, 89). It follows that the aim of parents should be to surround themselves with children who are allowed to get their own way to the degree that the peace of the family as a whole will permit. And it follows that, if the parents can't understand this wisdom, the children should at least try to get their own way in spite of them. It isn't easy. Ernest has been so thoroughly crammed with the doctrine that he ought to seek his parents' happiness to the exclusion of his own, that he begins his pilgrimage on his knees — the posture not just of the prayerful but of the force-fed. The more he can be persuaded that he too may be happy, that he has the duty occasionally to eat the fruit of the lotus, that, more importantly, he has an obscurely felt but still authentic destiny as a writer — the more he can be persuaded of these, the better. He needs as much *amour-propre* as he can get.

The response of many readers, however, is determined by the Ernest they remember at the end of his story, and he, they say, has rather too much *amour* for himself. Of course there is no use denying that *amour-propre* can become narcissism and self-complacency, and that we see such a degeneration — or more accurately, such a failure to develop — in the older Ernest. But we ought I think to acknowledge that Butler initiates his hero's early rejuvenation according to the best lights of his moral tradition. Like everyone, Ernest requires what Hume calls "a due degree of pride," which is not to be confused with "over-weaning conceit," but is identical with valuing oneself aright. Better too much *amour-propre* than too little:

> 'Tis requisite [Hume writes] on all occasions to know our own force; and were it allowable to err on either side, 'twou'd be more advantageous to overrate our merit, than to form ideas of it, below its just standard. Fortune commonly favours the bold and enterprizing; and nothing inspires us with more boldness than a good opinion of ourselves.

The "bold and enterprizing" deeds of an Alexander were spurred by a just self-esteem, and accordingly Christian moralists discount his "virtues as purely pagan and natural," and by recommending the greater virtue of humility, they "[correct] the judgment of the world." Then, with precious irony, Hume concludes:

> Whether this virtue of humility has been rightly understood, I shall not pretend to determine. I am content with the concession, that the world naturally esteems a well-regulated pride, which secretly animates our conduct, with-

out breaking out into such indecent expressions of vanity, as may offend the vanity of others.

Amour-propre, "a well-regulated pride," is therefore the motivating power behind any worldly man's conduct, nor is it something he need hide, beyond the "appearance of modesty and mutual deference" which "the vanity of others" requires.[19]

That Ernest doesn't direct his *amour-propre* much beyond the practice of being (to say no more) a decent friend and a daring writer, does not mean that the moral postulates of *The Way of All Flesh* are incapable of yielding more. The realization of a life of fully active virtue — public spirited, domestically benign, sexually devoted, militarily heroic — depends on something which is not far removed from narcissism, but which is refined into magnanimity. Because we love fame, Hume argues, "... we bring our own deportment and conduct frequently in review and consider how they appear in the eyes of those who approach and regard us. This constant habit of surveying ourselves, as it were, in reflection, keeps alive all the sentiments of right and wrong, and begets in noble natures a certain reverence for themselves as well as others, which is the surest guardian of every virtue."[20] Effectual "reverence for...others" is hardly a function of free-floating sympathy. That is the error of Christian ethics, as Hume conceives them. Rather, sympathy and self-love function together as the twin innate particulars of human nature.

One could well object that my attempt, via Hume, to project a magnanimous ethics out of the postulates of *The Way of All Flesh* is merely academic — a case of special pleading — unless I can show more evidence of sympathy between and for other people in that book than, to gather from the published criticism, most readers remember. The first source of evidence must be Overton, who as narrator sets the norm for our expectations of the other characters. I shall say nothing of the massive sympathy he evinces in the very re-creating of the Pontifex history — the ability to put himself inside the consciousness of others, and — *tout comprendre c'est tout pardonner* — to tolerate their foibles. I shall instance only his conduct *vis-à-vis* his godson.

There is, to be sure, the side of Overton which, on the principle that one "should only consort with things that are getting their own way so far that they are at any rate comfortable," often concludes that he can do nothing for the uncomfortable Ernest — or chooses to say he can't (*WAF,* 89). There is another side of him, however, which is happily less sniffy. He relates a parable:

> I once saw a very young foal trying to eat some most objectionable refuse, and unable to make up its mind whether it was good or no. Clearly it wanted to be told. If its mother had seen what it was doing she would have set it right in a moment, and as soon as ever it had been told that what it was eating was filth, the foal would have recognised it and have never wanted to be told again — but evident though the matter was, still the foal could not settle the matter whether it liked what it was trying to eat or no without assistance from without. I suppose it would have come to do so by and by, but it was taking time and trouble, all which a single look from its mother would have saved.... (*WAF,* 218)

Overton realizes that occasionally the young foal Ernest needs a maturer horse to step in and set him straight, and eventually this is what he tries to do. Not content to be an invisible trustee of Alethaea's bequest, he intervenes with Towneley to help Ernest through his legal scrape; he sequesters him from his parents when they hunt for him after his release from prison; he tells him, to his immense relief, that he thinks his parents are horrid; he secures him and Ellen decent quarters for their business, and insists that he keep up his literary and musical habits in the meantime; he trains him in the rudiments of double-entry bookkeeping, the pace of foreign travel, and the enjoyment of light opera. And he is the interlocutor Ernest needs to work out the emotional and intellectual dilemmas his upbringing has brought upon him. More than the witty, iconoclastic, yet generally conservative gentleman we come to like as the narrator, Overton is a fair version of the good friend and counselor that Butler wished for in a father.

As Overton supplants Theobald in Ernest's life, so Alethaea, my second source of evidence of sympathy, supplants Christina. Ernest finds his godparents (who of course ought to have married but never did) to be more paternal and maternal than pater and mater are. Alethaea is mostly remembered for the huge legacy she leaves Ernest, which in thirteen years more than quadruples, on the strength of the new railways, to the gilded-age figure of £70,000. But she is a more complicated character than that. More purely than Overton, she manifests a capacity to be interested in the welfare of another — though the comparison needn't be to Overton's discredit: she is related to Ernest, he isn't. The blood-tie is important to her as she tries, unconsciously at least, to insure the happy survival of her family. She knows she can best serve her species by serving them.[21] I mean, of course, serving those of them who are "nice," if such there be. She goes to Roughborough to see whether Ernest qualifies; if he does, she will "exploit him" — i.e., use him as a depository for her money after her death. When she proposes to move to Roughborough to oversee the important part of his education, and thus to prepare him to use properly the money he shall have, Overton rightly asks:

> Was it a prudent thing to attempt so much? Must not people take their chances in this world? Can anyone do much for anyone else unless by making a will in his favour and dying then and there? ...
>   [B]ut against them [all these excellent reasons] there pleaded a woman's love for children, and her desire to find someone among the younger branches of her own family to whom she could become warmly attached, and whom she could attach warmly to herself. (WAF, 122)

She discerns at once that, for all his Theobald-bred priggishnesses, Ernest "likes the best music ... and ... hates Dr. Skinner; this is a very fair beginning" (WAF, 121). She picks out the nice boys and has them to tea, on the understanding that these youths — "She fell in love with one boy from seeing him put on his gloves" — are "much nicer...than those who profess to teach them," and will do more for Ernest's breeding than the Battersby sofa or the Roughborough refectory ever have (WAF, 125). Best of all, she introduces Ernest to carpentry, partly out of a belief that a boy ought to have a trade to fall back on (precisely what public school education doesn't give him), and partly out of a desire to see Ernest get some muscular exercise. It gives him the happiest time of his life. His aunt, for her part, "never gave him a syllable of good advice, or talked to him about every-thing's depending upon his own exertions, but she kissed him often and would come into the workshop and act the part of one who took an interest in what was being done so cleverly as ere long to become really interested." Soon Ernest's cheeks are flushed and his eyes glistening: "His inner self never told him that this was humbug as it did about the Latin and Greek. Making stools and drawers was worth living for, and after Christmas there loomed the organ, which was scarcely ever absent from his mind" (*WAF,* 129). Alethaea dies before Christmas and the organ is never built. Yet she leaves not only the legacy, but the sensible order that Overton wait till Ernest is twenty-seven before handing it over: he will need time to "go here and there, and learn his truest liking by finding out what, after all, he catches himself turning to most habitually" (*WAF,* 133). With his cramped heritage, he will not be ready to inherit £30,000 at the age of twenty-one, as his being fleeced by Pryer amply proves.

Besides the sympathetic examples set by the godparents, there is a third, that set by the godson himself. Most notably, he learns to identify with the sufferings of children, partly because his own sufferings have so strongly impressed themselves on him, and partly because he would not "offend . . . these little ones." He remembers *his* childhood as Theobald never was able to remember his own, and thus he recognizes very well what his children's lives would be like if they remained near him and Overton. The latter is too old to be bothered with scampering four-year-olds, and Ernest himself is too affectively exhausted to give them the on-going love they need. He sees with a clear but not a cold eye that the best thing for them is fosterage with a bargeman's family, among whom they will have the companionship of other children, the invigoration of the out-of-doors, and the prospect of a trade to enter into. None of this, as I shall discuss later, sufficiently solves the problems of child-rearing which Ernest's story has emphasized, nor does it ignore the apparent convenience which fosterage provides him. But it is not *just* convenient to him, it is also beneficial to the children. Ernest shows a capacity for self-transcendence which was lacking in his father, and which bodes favorably for future Pontifexes.

IV

We cannot measure the presence of sympathy in *The Way of All Flesh* without, finally, measuring it in Butler himself. "I may," he says, "very likely be condemning myself all the time that I am writing this book, for I know that whether I like it or no I am portraying myself more surely than I am portraying any of the characters whom I set before the reader" (*WAF,* 55–56). But it could not be simply a "condemning." The Butler we know from the biography was often extraordinarily generous in the friendship he gave men like Jones, Hans Faesch, and Alfred Cathie his servant. And from the writings we know how completely he could empty himself for the sake of bringing forward the Shakespeare of the sonnets, or the authoress of *The Odyssey*. The books expounded *his* theories, but on *their* behalf. The test case, however, is Butler's relations with Miss Savage, whom he first met at Heatherley's Art School and who was his best (and often it seemed his only) literary prompter and critic from the debut of *Erewhon* till her death in 1885. Without her, it is safe to say, we either would never have had *The Way of All Flesh* at all, or would have had it in the form of a treatise. I could iterate the humane criticisms she offered of the MS. as she read it, but my purpose is to note instead how she brought out what was humane in Butler the man. He relates an encounter with her which gives us some of our happiest glimpses of him — what he might have been like had he grown up with unpresuming people in the Italian Alps, rather than among the Butlers at Langar:

> I liked the cherry-eating scene too [referring to *Alps and Sanctuaries*] because it reminded me of your eating cherries when first I knew you. One day when I was going to the gallery, a very hot day, I remember, I met you on the shady side of Berners Street, eating cherries out of a basket. Like your Italian friends you were perfectly silent with content, and you handed the basket to me as I was passing, without saying a word. I pulled out a handful, and went on my way rejoicing without saying a word either. I had not before perceived you to be different from any body else.[22]

She could do this for him, and she would have done more if he had let her. But when she challenged him to commit himself emotionally and sexually to her, he showed the white feather — and he knew it. His notes on their correspondence are full of anguished remorse — denunciations of his own selfishness, feelings of helplessness about his inability to respond to her and marry her as she clearly wished.

There is no need to repeat the story Miss Savage and Butler have already told in the correspondence which Geoffrey Keynes and Brian Hill published forty-five years ago. It is enough to see that the fund of sympathy in Butler's life was if anything smaller than that in his novel; it was not so trifling as Malcolm Muggeridge would have us believe, but it was indeed pretty meagre. He had come of age terribly wounded, with a hunger for affection and an atrophied power for giving it, that marked him till he died. Witness, concludingly, the picture he gives of himself in a letter to Hans Faesch:

17 April 1895 — I travelled from Patras to Athens with a young Turk, about 30 years old, and his dog — an English terrier. We were alone in the carriage the greater part of the time, and I suppose the poor dog was bored, at any rate after a while he made up to me; he licked me all over my face, and then began to pretend that my coat pocket had got a rat in it which he must catch. I was so flattered at being made up to by anyone or anything who seemed to tell me I was a nice person that I let him go on and hunt for rats all over me, till at last his master interfered in beautiful English and then we talked. He was a Secretary to the Turkish Legation and was very clever and very nice.[23]

Edmund Gosse misses the tone of this letter when he says that here was a man who, "though love was in his heart, was forever out of harmony with the world, and suspicious of those whom he would fain have ingratiated."[24] Out of harmony, yes, but suspicious? Not in this case, surely; and when we think of Pauli, we know that in other cases he was not suspicious enough. Poor Butler wanted so much to be loved that he was grateful for the licks of an English terrier, and happy to have met a Turkish swell. "[A]nyone or anything who seemed to tell me I was a nice person": we are reminded of little Ernest, so grateful for the affection of puppies or kittens because he got none from mama or papa.

It is not surprising that a man whose sympathetic capacity had been so frustrated in his childhood should do no better in his adulthood than to know friendship with a handful of the living, and literary allegiance to a handful of the dead. He had no strength for tackling the larger problems of political economy and of marriage and the family. Those he bequeathed, as it were, to his spiritual heirs — Shaw, Forster, Lawrence. Yet — this is my point — whatever they contributed to our understanding of those problems rests on assumptions which Butler, himself continuing the moral tradition of Hume, had helped establish. The actual capacity for sympathy, without which neither the polity nor the family can be fruitfully addressed, may have been meagre in Butler and his work — though, as I have shown, it was greater than has been thought. But it was potentially as large as that of Hume, and it only needed writers of less hobbled genius to realize it.

Consider, for instance, the way Shaw extends Butler's ethics beyond the initiatory quarrel with parents and the whimsical defense of artistic reputations. Butler had tried to be wealthy in isolation, keeping Alfred on guard between the sanctuary of Clifford's Inn and the rest of London; Shaw knew that the wealthy man, for his own sake, must share his money with others. As Claude Bissell has written apropos of *Major Barbara*: "The socialist simply carries individualism to its full logical development. He cannot achieve peace, security, and contentment in isolation, for he will be constantly harassed by the spectacle of human suffering and degradation. Concern for others is the final form of concern for himself."[25] Butler would indeed have been interested in any political scheme which promised to lessen the harassments felt by men with full bellies. But like the author of *Back to Methuselah*, whose concern is less for the individual personality than for the "seed" reaching out toward a life of pure spirit, Butler desires the good of the race. *That* is what must flourish; if for abulic reasons it fails, the "One Life" of which it is part will bring forward a species that can and will do better. This concern for the collectivity, not for the monadic self, is, *pace* Mr. Bissell, "the Butlerian inheritance."

The dialectical relations between the collectivity and the self are patent in Butler's emphasis on the Pontifex family, his carefully tracing the bridges (*pontifex* means bridgemaker, according to folk etymology) between each of the five generations.[26] The well-being of any one member of the family depends very much on the well-being of the others. Ernest is "well" insofar as his aunt leaves him money, but he is still discomfited by the bad feeling between him and his parents. The great-grandfather John is "well" insofar as he pursues the arts and the charities which please him, but he is bewildered whenever George deigns to come home. And so on: what Butler understood about the principles of interdependence within the family, Shaw understood about the whole commonwealth. More, it is evident from the former's notebook entries on "good breeding" and from the latter's *longueurs* of dramatic fantasy that each could abstract the principles and apply them to the whole life of the planet.

The capacity for sympathy — embryonic in Butler, grown-up in Shaw — is central to their ethics, and both therefore share the influence of Hume. In the *Inquiry* especially, Hume insists that the public interest, though originating accidentally from the machinations of countless private interests, is *sustained* by man's powers of disinterested feeling — all that enables him to ask not just "What is it to me?" but "What is it to us?" Yet Butler and Shaw also stress a human capacity which Hume acknowledges with admiration, but which, perhaps because eighteenth-century science still let him take it for granted, he doesn't trumpet abroad. I mean the human intelligence. "Nothing is more vigilant and inventive than our passions," Hume writes in wonder at the spirit with which men put up restraints against their own acquisitiveness for the sake of that very acquisitiveness — the artfully roundabout way in which the institution of property enables them to secure in the end what they wanted in the beginning.[27]

Butler and Shaw emphasize the role of intelligence the more tellingly because, as we have already seen, Darwinism had negated it. What was clear to Shaw in the 'nineties was groaningly evident after the Great War: Europe could choose either the Darwinian mess of selfish competition, each man and nation alone, or the Lamarckian ideas of generous cooperation, each man and nation dedicated to the survival of the species. As Shaw writes in the "Preface" to *Methuselah*:

> Now all this [pre-war "diplomacy"] ... was fundamentally nothing but an idiotic attempt on the part of each belligerent State to secure for itself the advantage of the survival of the fittest through Circumstantial Selection. If the Western Powers had selected their allies in the Lamarckian manner intelligently, purposely, and vitally, *ad majorem Dei gloriam,* as what Nietzsche called good Europeans, there would have been a League of Nations and no war.[28]

Or as it is written in little in *The Way of All Flesh*, the struggle for the survival of the fittest in the Pontifex family means children who are stunted and "homesick," a mother who is an ambulatory reverie, and a father who thinks it a moral triumph to have brow-beaten his son into a confession of which boys at school "Will smoke next half," and which smoke already. And not just in the Pontifex family. Butler's several assurances that his story about them is simply a heightened (because immediate) instance of what one might find in countless families of an evangelical stamp, whether clerical or no, are certified by what we know of the households of the young Froude, Kingsley, Ruskin, Gosse, or John Addington Symonds. Those whom such households didn't destroy were left morbidly introspective and self-critical for the rest of their lives. It was high time for the neo-Lamarckian, the neo-Humean Butler and Shaw, champions of the power of our intelligence to change the way we live, to trumpet as they did. For what went on between husbands, wives, and children did indeed have much to do with what went on between classes and countries.

V

Enough said about the question of how much sympathy Butler's hedonism contains in practice, and how much in potential. What begins in Hume and culminates in Shaw is worthily mediated in Butler. I want to conclude my discussion of Butler's hedonism by addressing two directly philosophical attacks on it.

The first and most common is that made by, say, Peter Coveney when he writes that Butler leaves "unexplored the debatable ethic of unrestrained hedonism"; that his maxim concerning "the duty of seeking all reasonable pleasure, and avoiding all pain that can be honourably avoided" (WAF, 30), evades the hard question of what constitutes the reasonable and the honorable.[29] As we have seen, however, Butler hasn't evaded the question: the reasonable and the honorable are comprised of good health, toward which the organism is guided by its own discerning prudence — the intelligence that discriminates the balance of pleasure over pain which makes up happiness. Like Epicurus he abhors the "dishonor" of sickness; he understands that well-being comes from moderation, and that the ecstatic is beneficial only inasmuch as it stimulates a dulled sensibility back into action. Butler's own modest demands on life, his quiet enjoyments, are a model of temperance — and if corrective were needed, it would be in the direction of more ecstasy, not less. Mr. Coveney's bogey of "unrestrained hedonism" exists in neither the theoretical nor the practical ethics of Butler.

The more telling attack, which no critic has yet been philosophical enough to direct against Butler himself, is that which G. E. Moore, in the Principia Ethica, directs against hedonism as he finds it expressed in the utilitarian doctrines of Bentham and J. S. Mill. One can imagine Moore joining battle with Butler as follows: Bentham's hedonism was quantitative, measuring pleasure in terms of physiological sensation, and thus exalting the well-fed clam as the sort of creature we ought to emulate. You sound very much like an unreconstructed Benthamite when you have your doctor recommend that Ernest study the larger mammals at the zoo in order to rediscover the whole duty of man. Of course you have tried, like Mill, to advance beyond Benthamism by proposing a qualitative hedonism, whereby pleasures include not just physiological sensations, but psychological activity — the joys of contemplation, of aesthetic creation, etc. But you still cannot discriminate the value of one kind of pleasure from that of another. What makes psychological pleasure "better" than physiological? What makes a particular psychological pleasure — say, listening to Handel — "better" than another — say, admiring well-dressed women? The dilemma may be illustrated if we say that color alone is good. We find ourselves unable to establish the superiority of red above blue, or blue above red, for since both red and blue are colors, they are of equal value. We can only discriminate the *amounts* of red or blue — their intensity, their area, etc. — and so find ourselves falling back on a quantitative hedonics after all. If pleasure alone is good, then we must say with Bentham that "Quantity of pleasure being equal, pushpin is as good as poetry." If you find that an unacceptable proposition, your way out is to realize that different kinds of pleasure can be evaluated only by a criterion *other* than pleasure — namely, "the good." Finally, even if you are content to remain a Benthamite, you commit an error in logic which by itself betrays the folly of your position. You proceed illicitly from the presumed fact that all men seek pleasure (an indicative "is") to the declared law that their duty is to seek it (an imperative "ought"). You have derived the desirable from the desired, which is the more puzzling when, like Mill, you show yourself willing to admit that there is a difference between good and bad desires.[30]

How devastating are Moore's two criticisms of the Butlerian ethics? I think Butler would grant their consistency, but would find them irrelevant to the moral life as he perceived it. About the first criticism: we might well wish that there were an external good — a sort of qualitative hedonometer — by which we could weigh the value of one pleasure against another. But there is no such good. The *telos* of an organism is not dictated from without, by a deity or by an idea. It is created from within — conditioned indeed by tendencies and capacities inherited from organisms which made their own ends in ages past, but directed and adapted by the organism of the present. An organism doesn't gravitate toward *the* good; it partly finds, partly creates *a* good — one fit for it, one it likes for itself. Moore's ethics are transcendental, his good being undefinable because distinct from all phenomena. (His famous "naturalistic fallacy" is committed whenever one tries to compass the good within phenomena, i.e., whenever one tries to define it at all.) Hence his notion of *telos* is eschatological, an ultimate future an organism moves toward. The future, Butler would retort, is something we make: *telos* is an immanent idea, impelled from behind and steered here and now. About the second criticism: Moore's concern for the derivation of "ought" takes care of itself. The "ought" is contained within the "is" of our given instincts: i.e., our unconscious self, the chorused voices of our forebears, commands us to seek "all reasonable pleasure." We have a circle whereupon "ought" comes from "is" and "is" from "ought" — a circle whose starting point is unknowable, whose united processes of command and of performance should be analyzed only for the convenience of the story-teller: now Ernest listens to "the God who made [him]," and now he obeys.

One might suggest that the quarrel over the philosophical legitimacy of Butler's ethics would be obviated had he distinguished between "pleasure" and "happiness," making the latter the goal and the former its accompaniment. The hint is given by Aristotle, who says "everyone thinks [rightly] that the happy life is a pleasant life, and links pleasure with happiness" — happiness itself being the "excellent activity of the soul."[31] Pleasure is what we feel when we are doing the "excellent activity." We don't desire, say, aesthetic contemplation because it gives us pleasure; we get pleasure from aesthetic contemplation because it satisfies our desires.[32] But why, Butler would ask, do we desire aesthetic contemplation? What makes that more excellent than sensual gratification? The question of what constitutes excellence remains undecided, different philosophers offering different definitions. There is no final end in ethics, just as Ernest discovers that, since "no one could get behind Bishop Berkeley," there is "no [final] system based on absolute certainty" in metaphysics (WAF, 286). All the ethicist can (and need) do is to look at his own activities, and determine for himself which bring him the greatest happiness — which are accompanied by the greatest pleasure.

So we witness Ernest testing himself aesthetically and finding that he likes burlesque more than Shakespeare, Shakespeare more than the other Elizabethans, Aristophanes more than Aeschylus, and Aeschylus more than the Psalmist. Or vocationally, he finds he despises his work as a clergyman, wherein he must preach doctrines which he cannot upon examination believe, and must feel ashamed in front of the Methodists who beat him theologically, the tinkers who beat him hermeneutically, and the Towneleys who beat him sartorially. The work of a carpenter or a tailor, on the other hand, proves immediately satisfying: building stools and drawers is invigorating and useful, and as for good clothes — why, if he can't wear them, he can at least learn to sew them! Whether or not we regard Butler's ethics as more properly eudaemonistic than hedonistic, our practical emphasis must be upon the latter: the happiness of our "excellent activity of the soul" (or rather, of the body-soul) is determined by our sense of the pleasure which accompanies it. And that, in turn, is something *we* must judge from our own concrete experience: there is no abstract hedonometric chart to do the calculating for us.

Locke, Chesterfield, Cobbett, and Butler: The Theory and Practice of Education

Butler has clearly marked the source of opposition to his child-hero Ernest's struggle for integrity. It is the "long course of Puritanism [that] had familiarized men's minds with Jewish ideals as those which we should endeavour to reproduce in our everyday life." Prior to the Puritan revolution of the seventeenth century, relations between parents and children were apparently genial, as witness the fact that "The fathers and the sons [the legitimate sons, anyway] are for the most part friends in Shakespeare." But "Abraham, Jephthah [who sacrificed his daughter (Judges 11:29–40)] and Jonadab the son of Rechab [Rechab had forbidden his son to drink wine, plant vineyards, build houses, or farm fields (Jeremiah 35:6–9)]" offered dubious precedents to a civilization that assumed the inerrancy of the Bible's every word, and that found more specific advice about child-rearing within the writings of the Old Israel than within those of the New (*WAF*, 21). One can, for instance, imagine Christina doing an embroidery sampler of verses from Ecclesiasticus 30:

> An horse not broken becometh headstrong: and a child left
> to himself will be wilful.
> Cocker thy child, and he shall make thee afraid: play with
> him, and he will bring thee to heaviness.
> Laugh not with him, lest thou have sorrow with him, and
> lest thou gnash thy teeth in the end.
> Give him no liberty in his youth, and wink not at his follies.
> Bow down his neck while he is young, and beat him on the
> sides while he is a child, lest he wax stubborn, and be
> disobedient unto thee, and so bring sorrow to thine

> heart.
> Chastise thy son, and hold him to labour, lest his lewd
> behaviour be an offence unto thee. (vv. 8–13)

The nineteenth century saw a great change in parent-child relations, as the Romantic view of the child as innately innocent and vitally spontaneous exorcised the "ecclesiastical" view of him as innately depraved and lewdly willful. This exorcism was naturally slower to take effect in the homes of clergymen, the indoctrinated heirs of Puritanism, than in the homes of the rest of the middle class. The Way of All Flesh, as several critics have established, is a kind of mop-up operation against an enemy already driven into stuffy enclaves.[1]

The critics have, for the most part, concentrated on the progress of English Romantic attitudes from Blake's "girls & boys...On the Ecchoing Green," through Dickens's Paul Dombey and Pip, towards the "memoirs" of Butler and Gosse. I believe the more fruitful procedure is the one I have been following: to trace Butler's affinities with the English writers of the Enlightenment who, after all, helped prepare for the revolution in attitudes which the Romantics effected, and with whom Butler shares a certain temperament. He has more in common with their witty urbanity, their skeptical irreverence, and their political conservatism, than he does with the pastoral, earnest, evangelical, and often radical sentiment which frequently characterized the writings of the great defenders of childhood in his own century. I propose to look at the theory of Locke and the practice of Lord Chesterfield and, at the turn of the age, William Cobbett. The line Butler cuts might be said to begin with the theorist, and to pass somewhere between the two mutually alien but significantly bonded practitioners.

I

The seventeenth-century Puritans regarded the child as a handy dumping ground for adult feelings of guilt, a special repository for an original willfulness, filth, and lewdness which baptism did not so much clean now, as promise to clean by and by. Moreover, children were creatures no adult could feel empathy toward; youth-time was a distant shore which adults had long sailed away from, and they had no desire to return. Into the eighteenth century, however, one can find instances of adults trying to identify with the feelings of children. Richard Steele's remarkable attempt to imagine the sensations of a newborn is worth quoting:

> I lay very quiet; but the witch, for no manner of reason or
> provocation in the world, takes me and binds my head as
> hard as she possibly could; then ties up both my legs and
> makes me swallow down an horrid mixture. I thought it an
> harsh entrance into life, to begin with taking physic. When I
> was thus dressed, I was carried to a bedside where a fine
> young lady (my mother, I wot) had like to have hugged me to
> death.[2]

And so on with the infant's fear of falling when his cousin whisks
him up over her head, and his sufferings when the nurse changes his
napkins and sticks pins into his every joint. That Steele, or anyone
else in the eighteenth century, should dare to interest himself in such
post-natal mysteries was intellectually respectable because of the
theological, epistemological, and educational writings of Locke.

Locke's service on behalf of children comes under three heads.

1. He asserts in *The Reasonableness of Christianity* that the morality
of the ancients, though possessed of "some light and certainty," had
yet failed to give mankind "a perfect rule." And why? The *only*
specific example he forwards has to do with children: the ancients
thought they "could, without a crime, take away, the lives of their
children, by exposing them."[3] The attitude of Jesus toward children
was unique in a world where infanticide was as common as con-
traception and abortion are in our own. Locke's implicit appeal to
Jesus' "Suffer little children, and forbid them not . . . " shows not only
how pivotal this attitude could be for contemporary treatment of
children, but how pivotal it was for Christian ethics in general. Since
Butler's enemy is Puritan Christianity, we should pause a moment to
consider how shrewdly sensitive Locke was in going back to *The
Reasonableness of Christianity, As Delivered in the Scriptures,* as the
full title of his treatise runs. And we shall find that Butler's defense
of children after all recovers essential Christianity — or as he would
say, removes the false Christ for the true one. A pause may be the
more necessary insofar as historians of childhood usually conflate
Christianity with Puritanism. Lloyd deMause, for example, mistakes
altogether the significance of Jesus' invitation to the children in
Matthew 19:13–15.[4] He writes off the passage as an exorcistic laying
on of hands, thereby missing both the upholding of the child's
trustfulness and simplicity as a type for the believer ("of such is the
kingdom of heaven"), and the warmth of the parallel account in

Mark 10:13–16, which ends: "And he took them up in his arms, put his hands upon them, and blessed them." Here and elsewhere in the Synoptics (Matt. 18:1–6; Mark 9:36–37) Jesus is, in C. H. Dodd's words, "above the heads of his reporters." And like the disciples who at first rebuke the children, his apostle Paul refuses to take him literally. He construes "children" to mean the spiritually immature grown-up, milk-fed and gullible (see I Cor. 3:1 and 13:11; Eph. 4:14; Heb. 5:12–14).[5] When Locke, by contrast, takes Jesus literally with respect to children, he is trying, in one way at least, to realign Christendom with Christianity.

2. Locke's epistemology is committed to the view that the newborn child is a blank tablet upon which nothing has yet been written. The gift of life may be finite, but the child is under no "necessity of sinning continually" through some innate corruption of character. Locke does not explicitly deny the doctrine of original sin, yet some kind of Pelagianism must ensue from his epistemological commitment — as is evident when, in The Reasonableness, he insists that Adam's sin brought nothing but death upon his descendants, death meaning not "the corruption of human nature in his posterity," about which the New Testament is silent, but simply "a ceasing to be." "...[N]one are truly punished, but for their own deeds" — and there is nothing predestinately sinful about them.[6]

3. The child appears, then, to be relieved of the burden of original sin. Yet he possesses an innate temperament — a certain "natural Genius and Constitution." It seems that the blank tablets are made of diverse materials, taking and giving diverse impressions — just as the prints one pulls from lithographic stone are different from those pulled from copperplate. Locke writes: "God has stampt certain Characters upon Men's Minds, which, like their Shapes, may perhaps be a little mended; but can hardly be totally alter'd, and transform'd into the contrary." The educationist's task is to direct the God-given "genius" of the child towards the most virtuous and useful ends, much as, by "a gentle Application of the Hand," one turns the headwater of a river into desirable channels, and so determines its issue "at very remote and distant Places."[7]

Told that the child is father to the man, some parents undertook the great experiment of seeing whether the "remote" man might after all be more generous and placable in consequence of a more careful and "gentle" nurturing of the child. The parents in the eighteenth century who could effectively write about their kindly experiments are preciously few, however. As Butler remarks, the literary picture we commonly get from Fielding through Jane Austen suggests that "*le père de famille est capable de tout*" (*WAF*, 20) — the implication being "capable of anything bad." I wish to inquire into the paternal performances of Chesterfield and Cobbett, not just because they were capable of something good, but because each assumed that his offspring had potential for indefinite good *or* evil, depending on the exertions of those responsible for their upbringing.

II

"Sir Isaac Newton, Mr. Locke, and (it may be) five or six more, since the creation of the world, may have had a right to absence, from that intense thought which the things they were investigating required."[8] But young Philip Stanhope, Lord Chesterfield's natural son, could plead "no such avocations." He was not exceptionally gifted enough to become a philosopher, but he would do very well as a subject upon whom to test a philosopher's theory. If Locke was right, there was nothing pre-written about Philip's character; it could instead be written from scratch, the pen being lively first in his father's hand, and ultimately in his own. The metaphor is especially apt when we behold the voluminous letters which, like a shelf of encyclopedias, began falling on Philip when he was four years old, and kept falling till he died at age thirty-six. They were a kind of script for him to follow, or indeed, a kind of tattooing meant to be both beautiful and indelible.

Before turning to the particulars of Chesterfield's inscriptions, though, we should note the touching naivety with which he understands Locke's educational theory. Chesterfield supposes that if a child is a *tabula rasa*, then anything goes. Well, not anything, perhaps: one must admit he hasn't the stuff of a Newton or a Locke, but he might very likely be, say, the successful statesman his father hasn't quite been. All that is necessary is to make the right impressions, etc. Chesterfield seems (quite naturally) to overlook Locke's caution about the child's God-stamped "natural Genius and Constitution ... which ... may perhaps be a little mended; but can hardly be totally alter'd, and transform'd into the contrary." His insistent letter-writing may have something to do with his inability to accept his son's middling but honorable character as it has been given. Now, this is a naivety which Butler, even more than Locke, is free from. He stresses the degree to which one's character is pre-written in terms of one's forebears' instincts, habits, organs — all the armature which they clap onto one's curled embryonic self. Butler would, nevertheless, eagerly join with Locke and Chesterfield in their faith that *not all* is pre-written: let them disagree about how receptive the tablet's surface is, as long as they agree to stand for the possibility of its receiving for the good impressions that are intelligently made. It may require a long time to "take" — Chesterfield expects to turn Philip into a Cardinal de Retz in ten or fifteen years, while Butler knows it requires twenty-five to turn a Theobaldized prig into an Ernest whom his friends "do not ... wish ... greatly different from what he actually is" (*WAF,* 357), and many more to turn his descendants into something still better. But "take" the educationist's impressions eventually will.

There are occasionally dicta in Chesterfield which Butler would sternly disapprove of. George Pontifex's will-shaking comes to mind when we read Chesterfield's ominous, if not wholly sincere reminder to little Philip "that you neither have, nor can have a shilling in the world but from me; and that, as I have no womanish weakness for your person, your merit must and will be the only measure of my kindness." Yet he shows a certain gentleness when he adds that "I do not hint these things [though he has of course just hinted them] because I am convinced that you will act right, upon more noble and generous principles...," which is an assurance George never offers when his mind is on his money. Again, the faunish Butler would mock at Chesterfield's forbidding Philip to laugh: "...there is nothing so illiberal, and so ill-bred, as audible laugher." Finally, Butler would feel ambivalence shading toward loathing for Chesterfield's exhortations to winning: "When I was of your age, I should have been ashamed if any boy of that age had learned his book better, or played at any play better than I did; and I would not have rested a moment till I had got before him."[9]

The center of Chesterfield's program, however, is perfectly consonant with the main articles of Butler's and it is noteworthy that Locke, in his treatise on education which Chesterfield read, had already written down, in systematic form, their shared desiderata — the traits which constitute the gentleman. The good breeding which Butler would discuss in language both social and scientific is, in Locke and Chesterfield, strictly social. Take these nearly parallel statements, which would befit a courtier's handbook: "Courage in an ill-bred Man," Locke writes, "has the Air, and scapes not the Opinion of Brutality: Learning becomes Pedantry; Wit Buffoonry; Plainness Rusticity; Good Nature Fawning."[10] And Chesterfield: "The scholar, without good-breeding, is a pedant; the philosopher, a cynic; the soldier, a brute; and every man disagreeable."[11] The specifics of good breeding go in Chesterfield under the head of "*the Graces,*" the pre-Pauline meaning of which Butler, as we have seen, tries to recover. Chesterfield declares honestly enough that his love for Philip partly depends on his dress and manners, wherein any awkwardness offends, any grace invites. He tenders many precise instances of what awkwardness and grace consist of, yet he knows as well as Locke that the first is not a matter of simply failing to remove one's hat, nor the second of forming nice compliments at the proper moments. It is a matter of having or not having an elusive *je-ne-sais-quoi,* a confluence of what Locke calls "a due and free composure of Language, Looks, Motion, Posture, Place, etc. suited to Persons and Occasions, and...learn'd only by Habit and Use" — learned, Butler will add, till it *is* habit, a movement of consummate unthinking which Locke figures as the "falling ... [of] Skilful Musicians' Fingers ... into Harmonious Order without Care and without Thought." The sort of thought which *is* desirable is intimated by Locke's and Chesterfield's dislike of pedantry in the passages quoted several lines above. Locke urges the parent to give his child as much knowledge of the world's affairs "as he can bear":

> ...how much more use it is to judge right of Men, and manage his Affairs wisely with them, than to speak Greek and Latin, or argue in Mood and Figure: or to have his Head fill'd with the abstruse Speculations of Natural Philosophy, and Metaphysicks; nay, than to be well-versed in Greek and Roman writers, though that be much better for a Gentleman, than to be a good Peripatetick or Cartesian: Because those antient Authors observed and painted Mankind well, and give the best light into that kind of Knowledge [of judging men and managing affairs].[12]

The hierarchy of disciplines is plainly drawn, and it is pertinent that the places Locke allows the ancient authors are within those of morals and business, our spiritual and material conduct. Chesterfield's remarks on the substance and advantage of Philip's education are similarly concerned with both kinds of conduct, but he shows a larger interest in the delight of getting one's knowledge of the world from books that are beautifully written:

> A gentleman has, probably, read no other Latin than that of

the Augustan age, and therefore can write no other; whereas
the pedant has read much more bad Latin than good, and
consequently writes so too. He looks upon the best classical
books as books for schoolboys, and consequently below him;
but pores over fragments of obscure authors, treasures up the
obsolete words which he meets with there, and uses them,
upon all occasions, to show his reading, at the expense of his
judgment.[13]

Butler was himself a superb gentleman classicist. He was among the
last to be able to give a Latin oration at St. John's College chapel,[14]
and he translated both of the Homeric epics into a very idiomatic
English. As The Way of All Flesh demonstrates, however, he hated
pedantry as much as Locke or Chesterfield did, not just because
pedants happen to resemble Dr. Skinner, who "had learned everything and forgotten everything," but because the effort of pedantry
takes valuable time away from more useful tasks. That is why "the
nice people...forgot what [Latin and Greek] they had learned as
soon as they could...[Those languages were] very well in their own
time and country, but out of place here" (WAF, 103, 115). Butler's
translations of The Iliad and The Odyssey were meant to save literate
Englishmen the pain of mastering the "out of place," to give them a
poetic stimulus to an active life in the world, and thus, he hoped, to
shut the door on the Peripatetics, the Cartesians, the scholiasts, and
the Skinners once and for all.

To praise "the graces" is to command an outward conformity to the
tastes and conventions of those who will be looking at you. Chesterfield knows the value of a certain hypocrisy, a willingness to go along
with fashionable prejudices with regard to dress, religious worship,
and political preference. It is better, he says, cheerfully to comply
with customs you think are foolish, both because they can't be
reformed overnight and because, like the widespread feeling against
the Pope, the French, or the Jacobites, they actually promote the
scapegoating unanimity on which the good of the commonwealth
rests. For most practical purposes, Butler says, nothing serves so
well as the common cant and conventions of one's neighbors, and he
would concur with Chesterfield that if a man is acute enough to see
through them, he will be acuter still if he keeps his opinion to
himself. "Diogenes the Cynic [Chesterfield writes] was a wise man
for despising them [foolish customs]; but a fool for showing it. Be
wiser than other people if you can; but do not tell them so."[15] That is

precisely the maxim of the High Ydgrunites, the Erewhonians who both reverence and surpass the goddess Ydgrun (Mrs. Grundy), and who resemble the exceptionally liberal clergymen of the age who had read *Essays and Reviews* and *The Origin* and yet had to do their Sunday duties, as well as the lapsed or metamorphosed Christians like Butler himself.[16] They reverence Ydgrun inasmuch as they wish to conform and live at peace with their low and middling Ydgrunite neighbors: they will quarrel or flagrantly go their own way only when "conformity [becomes]... absolutely intolerable," and even then with reluctance, for "...most of their countrymen feel strongly about the gods, and they hold it wrong to give pain, unless for some greater good than seems likely to arise from their plain speaking." To themselves however they make no secret of how they surpass the goddess, in that they know her to be a mere abstraction, no matter how many her worshippers, and in that they know "they are brave, and Ydgrun is not": they *will* stand up against majority opinion if they are forced to, whereas being the shrine of that opinion defines what Ydgrun *is* (*E*, 158, 157).

The composite of attitudes I have been describing looks like the neo-classical age's ideal of gentility. It is an ideal which Hume and Edmund Burke also give substance to, and which may be caricatured as a desire not for the Baptist's "raiment of camel's hair, and a leather girdle," but for the courtier's silk and satin; not Rousseau's child of untamed Nature, but Castiglione's child of consummate civilization.[17] The High Ydgrunites "were gentlemen in the full sense of the word; and what has one not said in saying this?" (*E*, 157). Butler clearly believes he has said more than that they are replicas of the previous century's beau ideal, or of his own century's "best class of Englishmen." He believes he has adduced a standard of conduct which makes for a gentler, more civil life for everyone. The High Ydgrunite not only is free in the pursuit of *his* excellence, he provides a model for others' pursuit of *their* no doubt different excellences — a model first of all in the good-natured inconsistency with which he mediates his thoughts and actions. He thinks whatever he likes, but he doesn't try to impose his thinking even on himself, to say nothing of others. Some waywardness of brain and body must be put up with, for neither the self nor the commonwealth can survive persecution. The flesh *will* burn if it is not allowed to "marry"; the sect *will* foment rebellion if it is not allowed to meet. The High Ydgrunite is a model, second, in the shamelessness with which he will lie. This virtue is obviously related to that of inconsistency, but

one must understand one's occasional *obligation* to deceive: there is
no survival otherwise. As Butler biblically says, "I make it a rule to
swallow a few gnats a day, lest I should strain at them, and so bolt
camels. . . ." Just as the plover acts rightly when she "lyingly" feigns a
broken wing to lure us away from her young, so we are acting rightly
when we "lie" to protect our children, or anything else we might
treasure. God is not angry with the plover or with us; indeed it is he,
as a "whisper" within, who commands the lie, and "not once only,"
but habitually.[18] The High Ydgrunite is a model, finally, in the
generosity and charity with which he treats his fellows. Being "nice"
— we must remember the manly charge Butler gives that word, so
quaint if not priggish to us — being "nice" conduces more, among
our species at least, toward the survival of the self and the society
than the stunts of militarism ever can. Though Darwin himself saw
the usefulness of gentle cooperation in the human struggle for
survival, his followers tended to present him as an apologist for
every evil from prostitution to the Boer War. It is this brutalizing of
women and men which Butler's ideal of the gentleman, got from an
earlier age and developed in the light of his own, stands against. It
does so not by political action — Butler lost no sleep over the fate of
his prostitute, or over the careering of *his* nation's empire — but by
the promulgation of a human ideal which, if it is any good at all, can
offer a motive for those who are fit for political action, and who
believe that "the best class of Englishmen" ought to exclude no one.

III

Chesterfield and Locke wrote with the tacit understanding that "the
best class" is exclusive, and their dicta were often abused not just by
the aristocracy who wanted to keep pretenders out, but by the
middle-class who wanted to pretend. William Cobbett is refreshing
because he has no aspiration to live in Belgravia or in the great
country houses. He never truckles, never desires to raise his children
in order to enhance the status of his family — to boost them into an
idle life of cashing coupons. His interest is in his children's health,
handiness, and fortitude — the qualities which indeed mark *him*,
one of the most independent and therefore persecuted men in turn-
of-the-century England.

While Chesterfield left the direct care of Philip to his tutor, Cobbett
and his wife insist on doing themselves the work of dressing, in-
structing, and disciplining their children. Servants, tutors, or inter-
mediaries of any sort are but too likely to neglect them, as Cobbett

proves by citing numerous cases of infants being dropped to the floor or being left to wander into fires and wells. Only parental solicitude will keep sufficient watch. If he and Mrs. Cobbett are invited out, they don't leave the children home with sitters: they take them along, or if that isn't convenient to their hosts, one parent goes alone while the other (frequently Mr.) stays home with them. Nor, at home, are the children relegated to a nursery corner; they are part of the working center of the house. As Cobbett cheerfully says:

> Many a score of papers have I written amidst the noise of children, and in my whole life never bade them be still. When they grew up to be big enough to gallop about the house, I have, in wet weather, when they could not go out, written the whole day amidst noise that would have made some authors half mad. It never annoyed me at all.

Why should he hush them and spoil their fun? Their youth is theirs for enjoyment, and it is the only youth they will have. What is the use, Cobbett asks with Rousseau, of inflicting privations upon a child when he might die at the age of twelve, and die perhaps as a result of those privations? The question much impressed Cobbett when he was about to become a father, and he determined never to have to feel the remorse of having taken joy from any young one of his:

> I was resolved to forego all the means of making money, all the means of living in any thing like fashion, all the means of obtaining fame or distinction, to give up every thing, to become a common labourer, rather than make my children lead a life of restraint and rebuke; I could not be sure that my children would love me as they loved their own lives; but I was, at any rate, resolved to deserve such love at their hands; and, in possession of that, I felt that I could set calamity, of whatever description, at defiance.

Even his way of saying he would deserve his children's love is bluffly honest rather than offensively vain; it is not a demand toward them, but a declaration of his own responsibility.

The Cobbetts have no need of schools or teachers: the parents are eager to teach the children themselves. Nor are scolding and physical punishment required for the process, since parental approbation, encouragement, and, most of all, example suffice. The children want to learn to read and write because they want to be *like* their parents, who so obviously enjoy reading and writing. When the children pick up the books lying round the house, they are not gulled into thinking insipid romances the height of literary enjoyment. What, after all, will a child learn in *Tom Jones*, Cobbett asks, except the nastiness of sobriety, obedience, and frugality, and the genial rewards of wildness, disobedience, and squandering? Or what will he gather from "the punning and smutty Shakespeare['s]" *Henry IV* but that companionship with "debauchees and robbers, is the suitable beginning of a glorious reign?" No, the best books are useful, describing, like Cobbett's own, the methods of agriculture, the rules of grammar, or the malversation of politicos. When the children are not reading, they have no hunger to kill time with silly games of cards or dice: "We did not want to 'kill time:' we were always *busy*, wet weather or dry weather, winter or summer." While other children are made to recite Hamlet's soliloquy in front of companies of bored but dutifully admiring adults, each Cobbett child is tending his own "flower-bed, little garden, plantation of trees; rabbits, dogs, asses, horses, pheasants and hares; hoes, spades, whips, guns; always some object of lively interest, and as much *earnestness* and *bustle* about the various objects as if our living had solely depended upon them." And indeed each child's own living may one day depend on his being master of the objects of farm life, for they are too well taught the value of "*health*, the greatest of all things," even to wish to live anywhere but in the country. True, Cobbett's neighbors, and sometimes the weakening Mrs. Cobbett herself, will pester him to send the children to school where they can "learn something":

> "Bless me, so tall, and *not learned* any thing *yet*!" "Oh yes, he has," I used to say, "he has learned to ride, and hunt, and shoot, and fish, and look after cattle and sheep, and to work in the garden, and to feed his dogs, and to go from village to village in the dark." This was the way I used to manage with troublesome customers of this sort. And how glad the children used to be, when they got clear of such criticising people! And how grateful they felt to me for the *protection* which they saw that I gave them against that state of restraint, of which other people's boys complained![19]

I would like to go on with the Cobbett family, but I have said enough to indicate the sure, attentive, independent parent that Cobbett was, and to describe his sons for what they must have been — hardy Tom Tullivers who didn't misuse their sisters.

In some ways Cobbett's ideas about child-raising are the ones Butler's own are trying to catch up with. *The Way of All Flesh* begins and ends in a Cobbettesque spirit — the veneration of rural eighteenth-century parenting in the figure of Ernest's great-grandfather, and the sending of Ernest's own children back into the country, where they gallop with the bargeman's own: "They were like a lot of wild young colts — very inquisitive, but very coy, and not to be cajoled easily....[The bargeman's own boys] were hardy, robust, fearless little fellows with eyes as clear as hawks..." (*WAF,* 339). But in other ways Butler cannot drop the Chesterfieldian assumption that a gentleman defines himself by membership in a hereditarily wealthy class — the assumption at work when Towneley redoubles his efforts to aid the imprisoned Ernest upon learning that he is to "come into his aunt's money in a few years' time, and would therefore then be rich" (*WAF,* 236).

Butler is caught between the *rentier* prejudices of Chesterfield and the populist iconoclasm of Cobbett. He was both too comfortable and too uninformed to question the former, but — in part because he *was* so comfortable — he never feared to emulate the latter's unceasing combat against bad faith and bad works among the intellectuals of his time. It is significant that Ernest, once he is out of prison, wants nothing to do with pretensions to gentility: "What has being a gentleman ever done for me except make me less able to prey and more easy to be preyed upon? It has changed the manner of my being swindled, that is all" (*WAF,* 316). Furthermore, after he has come into his money, he wants to give up the charade of hobnobbing with his fellow *rentiers,* even Towneley himself, because they are precisely the parties he must offend as he composes his tracts on marriage and inheritance laws. And as intellectual independence derives largely from the physical environment and the psychological expectations within which one grows up, Ernest reaches out to imagine conditions more salutary than those he has known as a child: not dining room and dormitory, but river and fields; not the standard professions of clergyman, doctor, lawyer, which the public schools and Oxbridge lead to, but the solidly useful trades of carpenter, tailor, musician, sailor, hotel-keeper, tinker, bargeman — all the alternatives which Ernest's Odysseyan education, intent upon "the ways and farings of many men," has given him glimpses of (*WAF,* 301).

Butler himself jumped off the professional treadmill first by becoming a sheepherder in a New Zealand that had been deflowered by Europeans only nine years before, and then by returning to England to study painting. But he found that either occupational experiment required capital: his father gave him some £4500 during his New Zealand venture, and the profits from it comprised the fund he lived off while studying at Heatherley's and writing unmarketable books. Obviously, he sent Ernest through imprisonment and apprenticeship as a tailor in order to repeat in London what he himself had experienced "at the back of beyond" in New Zealand. And to render him the advantages of his own inherited capital — indeed to multiply and hasten those advantages — he gave him Aunt Alethaea's bequest, the sum of which puts him on a financial footing so superior that he needn't associate even with other rich men. For a young man who has grown up under Theobald and Christina; who has no opportunity to crawl back into another mother's womb that he might be called out by a different father; who cannot unschool himself and become a truly competitive carpenter or tailor — what alternative is there but to come into a legacy, or to commit the Theobaldian suicide of seeking an obscure curacy in an indulgent Church? Aunt Alethaea's bequest is an unsatisfying, fairy-tale sort of solution which, instead of lulling us into the romantic reverie which was some popular novelists' stock aim, alerts us to the extremity of the problems which mere money is supposed to fix. What is called for is a more detailed investigation of Butler's prescriptions for child-rearing which, though they involve money as the means for acquiring material necessities, transcend the smug wisdom of the lottery winner.

The Educated Ego

The Erewhonian myth of pre-existence may be read at two different levels. On one, it is an amusing *reductio* of the Church's "legal fiction" of original sin: birth is the result of a criminal blunder on the part of the pure spirit who desires to put on flesh, in expiation for which he is forced to sign, by proxy, a statement admitting the depravity of his wish to come into the world, and enslaving himself to his parents in payment for their trouble in having him — the whole procedure being "confirmed" in a ceremony at age fourteen. On a second level, the myth is a serious, quasi-Platonic version of a truth darkly understood in the Christian doctrine of original sin and analyzed by some psychoanalysts in their discussion of birth trauma: namely, that being born *is* calamitous. Not that it is a literal fall from the realm of pure spirit into the realm of matter: a spirit or an intelligence — the words are synonymous for Butler — doesn't exist until sperm and ovum meet and a new organism gets under way. It is instead a fall from life in the womb, where one knows perfectly what's what and where all necessary provisions are piped in, into the life outside, where one must build one's own establishment in the face of strange contingencies and at the not always tender mercy of grown-ups. A myth about this sort of fall is no mere elaboration of a pointless lament: it is a valuable attempt to tell what goes "wrong" at birth, in order better to comprehend, once the irrevocable has happened, what the duties of child and parents are.

Having made the binding decision to be born, the child's duty clearly is to stay at his post and try to realize the amenities of life in the womb in terms appropriate to the new life outside. That doesn't mean a return to the fetal sleep. It means an active engagement with the different conditions of pleasure which the extra-uterine world sets. As the counselors in the realm of pure spirit are supposed to say to the departing: If you recall the bliss of your prior state, if, suicidally, you yearn for it as Orpheus yearned for the fading Eurydice, then "...fly — fly — if you can remember the advice — to the haven of your present and immediate duty, taking shelter incessantly in the work which you have in hand." The work the child has in hand is that of securing his own happiness, a work which, as we shall see, breaks down into a number of relatively simple "jobs." It is the parents who have the larger and more complex duty, appropriate to their opportunity to do something to repair the calamity that has befallen their children. They are "to remember how they felt when they were young, and actually to behave towards their children as they would have had their own parents behave towards themselves" (E, 173, 175). One usually images the golden rule's "Do unto others" as though the "others" were grown-ups. Butler suggests that they might also be children, which is to stretch the grown-ups' powers of empathy in directions that had been too strange for the Twelve, and have been too strange for the millions since. And no wonder. "For [though] all children love their fathers and mothers, if these last will only let them...," and though parents do often have an instinct to "let them" love, there is "no talisman in the word[s] 'parent' [or 'child'] which can generate miracles of affection," nor can affection be compelled by law (FH, 8; E, 176). Affection must be earned by both parties. That is their final duty, which they have a good, if rarely perceived, incentive to perform: in affectionate families the father of fifty and the son of twenty are friends, and the father of sixty doesn't feel that the son of thirty is impatient for him to die.

I

I want first to consider in some detail the child's "present and immediate duty," asking not only what must be done, but what faculties are needed to do it. "What shall I do?" This particular interrogative is several times on the lips of lawyers and plutocrats who want to know from Jesus how they shall inherit eternal life. Without reference to inheriting anything, it is what the conscience-stricken Jews ask of Peter when he tells them that the man they crucified has been made "both Lord and Christ" (Acts 2:36–37), a passage which Bunyan alludes to at the end of the first paragraph of *The Pilgrim's Progress*, where Christian, burdened by his sins and their wages, "brake out with a lamentable cry, saying, *What shall I do*?" There are, as many readers have noticed, several incidental parallels between *The Pilgrim's Progress* and *The Way of All Flesh* — the motif of a "progress" along a "way," Butler's early thought of calling his hero "Christian," the series of helpers through various trials, etc. — but the essential parallel is here, in the distress of asking how one is to escape death and come to life. And on the surface, Bunyan and Butler give the same answer: one must forsake one's kin, for the gate leading to the celestial city is too strait to admit a family crowd. Only the lean individual can fit through.

In the first half of Bunyan's book Christian has forsaken his wife and children, who see the light in the second half; in Butler's book it is the child who must forsake his parents and siblings, who never see the light. One must give up *all* for Christ, whether they follow one's lead or not. Bunyan has in mind Jesus' saying that "If any man come to me, and hate not his father, and mother, and wife, and children, and brethren, and sisters, yea, and his own life also, he cannot be my disciple" (Luke 14:26). Butler has the same saying in mind, but by identifying Christ, as we have seen, with the inward intelligence of "his own life," he radically changes Bunyan's (and Luke's) meaning. The coincidence of theme breaks down when we come to particular theologies; yet Luke, Bunyan, and Butler are tied together by the surprise, not to say the disgust, with which the ordinary reader hears the command to "hate" the near ones whom he is usually told he should love. Luke or Bunyan would be quick to explain that he is telling the believer to subordinate all to one goal, which is incorporation with Christ. With rather extensive transvaluation of terms, Butler ultimately gives the same explanation, but he fills in the immediate details more than either Luke or Bunyan is concerned to do. He says, in effect, that a man is to hate his family because they are devouring his soul between morning business and evening prayers.

Butler's rule of thumb is that one should never trouble to learn anything till one has been made very uncomfortable for a very long time by not knowing it. After such a wide invitation to quietism, his injunction to learn something as desperate as the severing of family ties — the giving up of that which ought to be a present help — indicates a situation which must be *very* uncomfortable, wherein the family members' duty of earning one another's affection has been altogether shirked. The trouble in the Pontifex family lies precisely in the parents' over-insistence on *being* a present help. They don't let Ernest do anything for himself, because they regard him as a mere duplication of themselves — or if he isn't, he ought to be.

Theobald expects the infant Ernest to be a "full grown clergym[a]n — of moderate views, but inclining rather to Evangelicism." When he finds that the boy is at first nothing of the sort, but only a squirming amalgam of Pontifex and Allaby juices, he drives him into the rectory greenhouse, weeding out all signs of self-will in order to cultivate a little J. S. Mill minus the radicalism: "Before he was three years old he could read, and, after a fashion, write. Before he was four he was learning Latin, and could do rule of three sums" (WAF, 79). Ernest refuses to be forced. He first quarrels with his father and pitches his own tent when, as a fetus, he attaches himself to the uterine wall. And once the umbilical cord has been cut, he may be said to have begun his quarrel with his mother too. He wants to have a separate self, but it takes him years consciously to realize that he does, and years more to realize that he *ought* — the latter illumination beginning at Roughborough when he puts the torch to Theobald's effigy, and culminating in London when he hears Overton say that his parents are awful. There is no contradiction, Jerome Buckley notwithstanding, between Butler's emphasis on the influence of heredity and his emphasis on the need for differentiation.[1] Ernest is continuous with his parents both biologically (their genes are his) and socially (their naivety and religiosity are his), but he is also separate from them. Biologically, it is *his* stomach that must be fed; socially, it is *his* emotions, *his* purposes that must steer his life as he moves into waters beyond his parents' ken. Theobald assumes that, since "ordination was the road [he] knew and understood, and indeed the only road about which he knew anything at all," then it must be the one for Ernest, too (WAF, 174). Such a road will lead Ernest into his grave. He must live his life as a good metaphor lives its life, by functioning within a convention, yet being sufficiently strange to stand out against it. If he repeats the convention and no more, he is dead.

What does Ernest require to stand out against his parents? As I have intimated, he requires luck, in both its circumstantial and its biological aspects. He also requires cunning — the power of intelligence which a) is one form of biological luck, b) is activated by circumstantial luck, and c) is free to improve upon both. Let us look at these requirements more closely.

Ernest's circumstantial luck comes to him in the external stimuli of Towneley's triple *No*'s, of Mr. Shaw's lesson in Form Criticism, of a pleasant six months in jail, of the glorious £70,000, and so on. These stimuli appear to be a series of lottery numbers, Ernest seeming less to have purchased the winning tickets than to have had them thrust into his hands. Lacking the fortitude and energy necessary to create his own advantages, he can only stand and wait: "He should not have had the courage to give up all for Christ's sake, but now Christ had mercifully taken all; and lo! it seemed as though all were found" (WAF, 260). If this apparent predestinarianism were everything, Ernest's break-through wouldn't be as interesting as it is. But "Christ" is no external deity whose last resource is shock treatment — the golden, amnesiac lightning which obliterates the awful Battersby past and makes possible a blessed, fairly unprescribed future. Rather, "Christ" is Butler's nonce-word for the unconscious intelligence Ernest's biological luck has given him. His "Christian" knowledge consists of his instinct for what gives pleasure, and his impulse to put himself into situations where he is likely to get it. "Christ" deflects his course into opportunities disguised as predicaments, wherein the "all" which hinders his seeking his own truest happiness will be swept away.

Think of the particulars of the Miss Maitland episode which precipitates Ernest's imprisonment. He advances upon her as he supposes Towneley to have advanced upon Miss Snow, trying thus to satisfy a hunger that is at once sexual and spiritual — to spend himself inside a woman, and thereby to achieve something of the lightness and eager virility of Towneley, who has "come before [his] time" with "a hurried step ... [which] bound[ed] up the stairs as though ... the force of gravity had little power" over him. "Christ" knows that these satisfactions can be got only by kicking into the corner "the Bible given him at his [false] christening by his affectionate godmother and aunt Elizabeth Allaby," and by marching off straight to do what the Bible forbids. "Christ" doesn't know tactically how to proceed beyond this — to determine, e.g., whether Miss Maitland is really like Miss Snow, as Mrs. Baxter says, or whether, as Mrs. Jupp says, she isn't (WAF, 231). Tactical knowledge is important, but it is secondary to the unconscious conviction that the restraints of clerical respectability must be cut. It is not too much therefore to say that Ernest's unconscious self drives him to an extremity wherein he either will commit the fornication he longs for, or will land himself in jail — which institution will effactually defrock him, that he might seek his satisfaction with a lighter tread. Nor do I think it too much to say that his unconscious self is what prompts him to ask Towneley whether he doesn't like poor people — a question which his conscience may suppose to be a righteous challenge, but which in fact is a request for Towneley to set that conscience straight by showing him how nobody is nicer for being poor, etc. Finally, in the conversation with Mr. Shaw it is Ernest's unconscious self which urges him to wield his conscience's greatest weapon, the Bible, to see how strong it actually is. He is like a man driving hard an engine he really wants to break — so that he can go get a new and different one.

One would be going too far in attributing so much cunning to the curate's unconscious self, were it not that the child's has shown so much already. When Ernest is ill and is encouragingly told by mama that he needn't be afraid of dying because, if he promises never to vex papa anymore, he will go to heaven and be with Grandpapa Pontifex and Grandmama Allaby and sing beautiful hymns to Jesus, he feels no "wish to die, and was glad when he got better, for there were no kittens in heaven, and he did not think there were cowslips to make cowslip tea with" (WAF, 83). He enjoys the things of this life very well: he is not going to be easily tricked into preferring those of some other. Then there is his reaction to his first meeting with Dr. Skinner, whose office is lined with books two rows deep "from floor to ceiling": "It was horrible" (104). And a while later Ernest provides himself an escape from Dr. Skinner's factious talk by beginning to cry — "doubtless through an intense but inarticulate sense of a boredom greater than he could bear" (106). At school he shirks fights of every species, including football, because, as "a mere bag of bones, with upper arms about as thick as the wrists of other boys of his age," and with a "pigeon-breasted" "little chest," he always gets beaten up (113). He despises himself for shirking, assuming that "the timidity natural to childhood" is evidence of his "cowardice." But in truth "the instinct which made him keep out of games for which he was ill adapted was more reasonable than the reason which would have driven him into them" (114). In the same way he avoids the sofa conversations offered by his mother, not because he is a worse coward than his fellows, but because "all sensible people are cowards when they are off their beat, or when they think they are going to be roughly handled" (153). It is precisely this discretion which rescues him from his parents' inquisition, as it has from Dr. Skinner's miasmal pleasantries: Theobald and Christina probe and probe into the misdemeanors of the Roughborough boys, "till they were on the point of reaching subjects more delicate than they had yet touched upon. Here Ernest's unconscious self took the matter up, and made a resistance to which his conscious self was unequal, by tumbling him off his chair in a fit of fainting" (163).

"*Sapiens suam si sapientiam nôrit*" (114): the young Ernest usually does know his own wisdom, but rarely can he articulate it. Dwelling within him as deep as it does, it ultimately defies full articulation, though the copious essays which interrupt Butler's narrative prove that it can be pointed to — articulated in approximate terms which are quite sufficient. In young Ernest, though, even approximate articulation is shouted down by the voice of his father — his "conscious self ... begotten of prigs, and trained in priggishness." This "outward and visible old husk" may do all the talking for a while, but it has no vital influence on Ernest's actions (116). Vital influence belongs to the unconscious self, inward and unseen, which is "the God who made [him]."

Butler's distinction between selves is of course analogous to that which Freud draws between the parties flanking the conscious ego: the conscience above ("super") and the id below. The Freudian terms are useful. What Butler calls Ernest's "conscious self" is what we should call his "conscience," though he is indeed so dominated by the voice of his father that in him the two are identical. But the psychology Butler is anticipating is less Freud's than Lawrence's. The issue is between those who regard the unconscious as rapacious and heedless, an energy which is necessary but always in need of governance, and those who regard it as moderating and trustworthy, an energy which, as long as novel dilemmas don't put it off the scent, can govern itself. Lawrence writes: "The Freudian unconscious is the cellar in which the mind keeps its own bastard spawn. The true unconscious is the well-head, the fountain of real motivity," which in its pristine state one knows not through concepts, but wholly and directly, as one knows the sun, or one's mother, or anything primal, the senses reaching out and "lovingly roving like the fingers of an infant or a blind man over the face of the treasured object."[2] One cannot, however, just live in intimacy with one's unconscious self, like an infant eternally at his mother's breast. When novel dilemmas arise, as they assuredly will, one needs an intelligently conscious ego, not just to hear the demands of the now bewildered unconscious, but to chart a course which will satisfy them. The conscious ego in Ernest's case is the implied addressee of the speech on p. 116. Butler is emphatic about the intelligence of the unconscious self, and I have suggested how Ernest's pushes him into situations where, one way or other, the obstacles between him and his richest pleasures will be cleared away. What Butler leaves to implication is the need someone as distressingly placed as Ernest must have for a shrewd ego to act as prophet for the "Christ" or "God" within.[3]

Consider how Ernest's conscious ego performs "God's" work. At Roughborough he wittingly schemes to sell an old Sallust in order to buy copies of the Handel oratorios. He chooses to aid the other boys in burning his father's effigy, thus "confirming" his election as "the huge old bishop" who has visited the school that day never could. At Cambridge he allows "God" to find out what aesthetically he really likes, and then articulates it, thereby completing the movement from taste, the province of the unconscious, to criticism, the province of the ego. Most notably, he decides upon leaving prison that he won't see his "most dangerous enemies," his parents, and when they outwit him by showing up in the receiving room, he firmly commands his father not to speak to him, and scrambles away. This crossing of the Rubicon is "not perhaps very heroically or dramatically" done, but done it is, with an effort which causes Ernest, once he is outside, to lean against the prison wall and weep (WAF, 263–64). It is a crossing that is demanded by "God," and effected by his prophet — an act of deliberate rebellion which has moved even the grudging Arnold Kettle to admiration, and which proves that "God" will be unseeing as well as unseen till he has an "I" who can watch and act for him.[4]

Do the decisions of the intelligent ego therefore accumulate toward the formation of a new superego? In some ways it seems so: Theobald and Pryer are replaced by Overton and Towneley, new objects of emulation. But that is only a psychologically convenient first stage (see above, pp. 42–43). The true conscience is not above the ego, but below it: the conscientious man lives in obedience to the divine commandments of his provident unconscious. And Ernest's unconscious is finally different not only from Towneley's, as we have noted, but from Overton's. As the latter's name suggests, he is "super" to Ernest — a figure who is obviously more congenial to him than Theobald, yet who must also be surpassed. Ernest must, for instance, write the serious theological and moral tracts which his own genius needs to write, and to do so in spite of Overton's call for something more entertaining. His unconscious self can't be entertaining till he has slain his enemies. Butler then is portraying a psyche which, in its healthy state, is not the tripartite affair which Freud portrays, wherein the ego strives to achieve a balance of power between its partners. It is a bipartite affair between the ego and the unconscious, the latter having a trustworthy wisdom of its own which renders a superior "governour" unnecessary. In someone like

Ernest the role of the ego is substantial: it is uncomfortably circum-
stanced and must be as conniving as it can. In someone like Towneley, though, the ego has very little to do: it is so well set up that it
can cruise on automatic pilot.

It isn't till Ernest is fairly grown that his ego displays any intelligence. When he is very young, it is at the mercy of his father's voice,
and he has to rely on his unconscious self to pull him out of scrapes
— whether by crying or by fainting. At one moment his inchoate ego
may feel righteous in disobeying his father, but at the next it feels
overwhelmed by its utter depravity. It won't be secure till, years later,
it has succeeded in locating its true conscience. It is to grown-ups,
therefore, that Butler is usually speaking when he pronounces the
do's and don'ts of family life. In a still more or less Puritan culture,
they alone have lived long enough perhaps to have seen through the
false divinity and to have got acquainted with the true, the inscape of
the self. They are in a position to avoid the mistakes made on them,
and from the beginning to promote with their own children the
message of Psalm 82: though "ye shall die like men," yet "Ye are
gods; and all of you are children of the most High." What Shaw
called a ceremony in "parricide [sic] and matricide long drawn out"
is then also a program against infanticide, no less drawn out.

II

What practical things should grown-ups do for the "children of the
most High" who are their charge? They should guide them in matters of money and sex, the bivium, so to speak, of the Butlerian
university, the branches of which we must discuss first separately,
then together.

Parents should give their children lots of money, or if no large
legacy can be brought together, give them the sort of training that
will put them in the way of making money for themselves. Butler is
sure that the individual talent, properly tutored, will rise to its own
level in the marketplace. But proper tutoring is precisely what the
English public schools and ancient universities don't provide for the
youth who must earn his own living. Dead languages, abstract
mathematics, far-away history, and Church dogmatics are certainly
not taught for their utilitarian value; nor, Butler feels, are they taught
especially for their "own sake" (whatever that would mean: what is
Latin, that it should have a sake?). Rather, they are just the sorts of
complex superfluities which are expensive and difficult to acquire,
and which therefore are the perfect signs whereby one can distin-

guish the quality from the commoner. So much the worse for the quality: such an education is costly to the parents, who naturally resent the drain on their capital, but more costly to the children, whose "retreat" is thereafter cut off. They can no longer turn to a trade or to manual labor, which alone could secure their independence (*WAF*, 23). Because Ernest's training in carpentry is aborted, he has nothing to fall back on when his curacy and his money are gone. He does train as a tailor in prison — luckily he is still young and eager enough to learn — but as Overton's own tailor Mr. Larkin sees, it is too late for him to begin. A public school boy can't be happy mixing with tailors, nor they with him: "A man must have sunk low through drink or natural taste for low company before he could get on with those who have had such a different training from his own" (269). That sentence may sound like quintessential Victorian snobbery, but in fact it points to a psychological reality that keeps most people from being more than theoretical egalitarians.

Butler joins a chorus of Victorians — Macaulay, Carlyle, Kingsley, Froude — who insist that education be materially useful; young people who have no great property coming to them, the majority after all, must get from their masters the know-how to enable them to earn honest livings. Even if a boy stands to inherit an independence, Butler argues, apprenticeship in a trade would still be prudent, for who knows what will happen at the "place they call the stock-exchange"? Moreover, a good grounding in economics will help him *look out* for what will happen there, and protect himself against the worst. Overton gives Ernest a belated introduction to the rules of double-entry bookkeeping ("the most necessary branch of any young man's education after reading and writing"), which is indeed but the instrument for the profounder art of speculation. Butler would have a course in speculation taught in every public school, the boys reading the financial papers and playing a sort of Monopoly with pence standing for pounds: "There might be a prize awarded by the headmaster to the most prudent dealer, and boys who lost their money time after time should be dismissed." Such a course might be continued at university, except that it would entail the creation of a professorship in speculation, and nothing that the universities do well — cricket, rowing, cooking — is taught by professors. So the course had better end at the sixth form (*WAF*, 302).

Butler is not jesting, nor, as far as the training of young *rentiers* goes, should he be. He is echoing the sound advice Locke offers on teaching boys the details of estate management — advice worth quoting at length:

> Many Fathers, though they proportion to their Sons liberal Allowances, according to their Age and Condition; yet they keep the Knowledge of their Estates, and Concerns from them, with as much reservedness, as if they were guarding a secret of State from a Spy, or an Enemy. ... Nothing cements and establishes Friendship and Good-will, so much as *confident Communication* of Concernments and Affairs. Other Kindnesses without this, leave still some Doubts: But when your Son sees you open your Mind to him, when he finds that you interest him in your Affairs, as Things you are willing should in their Turn come into his Hands, he will be concerned for them, as for his own; wait his Season with Patience, and Love you in the time, who keep him not at the distance of a Stranger. This will also make him see, that the Enjoyment you have is not without Care; which the more he is sensible of, the less will he envy you the Possession, and the more think himself Happy under the Management of so favourable a Friend, and so careful a Father.[5]

Neither George nor Theobald Pontifex has read Locke's book: whenever money is at issue between them and their sons, they can only clutch and threaten. George's favorite threats are to say that he will apprentice his boys to greengrocers, which they wish he would, or to shake his will at them, which they wish he wouldn't: "He would in his imagination cut them all out one after another and leave his money to found almshouses, till at last he was obliged to put them back, so that he might have the pleasure of cutting them out again next time he was in a passion" (*WAF,* 24). Theobald follows suit, though by shaking his will a little less, he perhaps a little more makes the rudiments of allowances, inheritances, and yearly expenses greater mysteries than they are.

"[M]ake no mysteries where nature has made none..." (169). The violation of that commandment with respect to money is discomfiting to Ernest both when he must go without his "*menus plaisirs*" at school and when he is shorn clean by Pryer in London. Its violation with respect to sexuality, however, is ruinous to him. Aunt Alethaea has wrapped a nest egg with Bank of England notes, to be kept warm for Ernest till he is ready to be "born" at age twenty-seven, and Overton has taught him how to husband it. No one, however, can do

much for him sexually. As a schoolboy he has his bout of what Robert
Graves calls pseudo-homosexuality, yet about heterosexuality he is
completely innocent. Indeed, when the servant girl Ellen, who in
order to prepare for confirmation ought to have been studying the
routes of Paul's missionary journeys, is discovered to have got
pregnant and Ernest is momentarily suspected, he turns out to be
"not only innocent, but deplorably — I might even say guiltily —
innocent" (143). Innocence is what prevents him from distinguishing between the characters of Miss Snow and Miss Maitland, and
what, once he has been punished for that error, leads him to suppose
that the new-found Ellen is the right woman to help him: "I had
learnt as a boy things that I ought not to have learnt, and had never
had a chance of that which would have set me straight." It may be
that "Gentlefolks is always like that," as Ellen says, but Ernest is so
"like that," so "starving for something to love and lean upon," that he
can't detect that this particular female "something" is too gin-ridden
to hold him up for long (272–73). Like his father before him, he has
been kept from knowing any females besides his mother and sister.
At Roughborough he has been lectured on the sanctity of the spirit's
temple, and at Cambridge he has been denied both the opportunity
to see "abandoned" women, and the money to buy them:

> At night [the judge at Ernest's trial ironically says] proctors
> patrolled the street and dogged your steps if you tried to go
> into any haunt where the presence of vice was suspected. By
> day the females who were admitted within the college walls
> were selected mainly on the score of age and ugliness. It is
> hard to see what more can be done for any young man than
> this. (238).

Ernest's parents and masters have only been following the advice of
the best ecclesiastical authorities. And were they here to turn to the
secular pundits whose wisdom, as I have argued, contributed so
greatly to Butler in other matters, they would not be much better off.
    Locke had nothing to say about the sex education of young Eng-
lishmen. Throwing up his hands in disgust at how fast vice ripened
among schoolboys and indeed among the whole of Restoration
society, and planning for himself removal to America, he recom-
mended that boys be tutored at home, regardless of expense. Cobbett,
for all his earthiness, faced the problem no more squarely. Chesterfield, though also insisting that boys not be thrown into the vicious

company of other boys, was a little bolder about the vicious company of women: he got so far as to allow Philip to lay out money on Italian courtesans, as long as they were reputable. And *that* is the advanced position, the latitudinarian remedy for lust between the succubae of puberty and the chaste sheets of marriage. Exploitative and joyless, it is the path for sexual discovery which Butler recommends: while others close their eyes and immure their sons, he proclaims (very quietly, it is true) the satisfactions of well-heeled whoremongering. He ought to be credited with having the candor to acknowledge the need for sexual discovery, but pitied — if that isn't too impudent — for failing to acknowledge the need for sexual maturation, which involves a delicacy and a fidelity to which a carefully folded pound note to Mlle. Dumas, once a week for many years, does not answer.

III

Butler does little, then, to dissipate the mysteries surrounding the growing youth's sexuality. He does a great deal, however, to dissipate those surrounding his need for money, and it is worth returning to the subject, not only because it is ultimately linked with that of sexuality, but because in its own immediate terms it has been so frequently misperceived. Butler's constant calls for money from his swindling and long-lived father, the wish-fulfilling bonanza he contrives for Ernest, his insistence on allowances, legacies, and a pre-money education all go rather shrill in the ears of most readers. Like Mr. Micawber he resolves his personal crises into the question of whether he has enough money: if yes, he is content; if no, he is miserable. Other variables seem not to count.

In *The Way of All Flesh* the fathers and sons go to war over great expectations and greater expenditures; even friends first meet each other as if through a teller's window, as when Overton introduces himself to little Ernest by giving him and Joey twopence halfpenny to buy "sweeties," and waiting for them to figure out how to make change. Everyone with lots of money — Towneley, Alethaea, or Overton — is supposed prima facie to be affable, successful, and virtuous; even Ernest's father and grandfather are thus respected by their neighbors, and with Butler's general concurrence. Small wonder, therefore, that Edmund Wilson should complain that "five years after *Das Kapital*, eighteen years after Dickens' *Hard Times*," Butler's class prejudices deflected his powers of satire away from the evils of capitalism; or that Arnold Kettle should mockingly say that Butler's famous "common sense...finds its level at fifteen hundred a year";

or that Miss Savage should indomitably lecture him as follows:

> I call you a most unreasonble man. Let the poor stupid
> disagreeable people have the money (I think they very often
> do); they want it poor things. When you get that modest
> competence you speak of, I shall look upon you as defraud-
> ing somebody or other.[6]

Small wonder that these voices should be raised, yet Butler is hardly
as myopic as they suggest. He knows that, given nature's limited
resources, somebody's good luck in the struggle for existence entails
somebody else's bad: it is not his fault, it is the system's — meaning
by "system" not any particular economics, but nature itself. Butler is
aware of the tenor of the socialist critique of capitalism, which
decries "the unearned increment of land [values]," and which ought
to extend to the similarly unearned increment of railway stock (*WAF*,
303). But since inequities between the haves and the have-nots are
simply a function of the pressure of large populations on small
reserves, he takes them for granted and is happy that, for the time
being, the socialists are rating landowners instead of stockholders.
Yet though he isn't as toadyingly myopic as his critics imply, he isn't
as liberally far-sighted as he might be, either. He sees economics with
the eyes of a Victorian *rentier* — Wilson is quite right about that. He is
exceptional in his criticism of Darwin's metaphysical assumptions,
but drearily ordinary in his acceptance of the economic corollaries of
those assumptions which men like Charles Graham Sumner and
Herbert Spencer were cheerlessly formulating.

   Still, Darwin had something extremely valuable to teach Butler
about economics, something which Butler elaborated in ways that
went on to be valuable for others. Darwin taught him, in a word, that
economics is inescapable. Life on this planet is stubbornly material
— not totally so, as Darwin thought, but mostly so nonetheless. We
have got to live on *something* a year, and Butler's "money" is only a
summary word for those material goods which we will produce,
distribute, and consume according to whatever system we can
devise, but which, if we want to survive, we can't forego. Darwin
grounded this truth in natural science; Hume and Dr. Johnson had, a
century earlier, grounded it in associational psychology and social
ethics. Each formulation finds a place in Butler, and each is necessary because there are rich people who, preferring not to struggle for
their money, want the poor to find virtue in submission, and because

there are people, rich and poor, who, ashamed at having to live in the flesh, want us to be like them and find beauty in the spirit alone.

Hume speaks of our "natural" respect for the wealthy and aversion to the poor, based upon the pleasant "ideas" accompanying the one, and the unpleasant the other:

> When we approach a man who is, as we say, at his ease, we are presented with the pleasing ideas of plenty, satisfaction, cleanliness, warmth; a cheerful house, elegant furniture, ready service, and whatever is desirable in meat, drink, or apparel. On the contrary, when a poor man appears, the disagreeable images of want, penury, hard labor, dirty furniture, coarse or ragged clothes, nauseous meat and distasteful liquor immediately strike our fancy. What else do we mean by saying that one is rich, the other poor?

Hume knows perfectly well that wealth is no guarantee of virtue, and that one doesn't measure out esteem in proportion to income. Personally, one judges the characters of men according to their intrinsic qualities, not according to the "capricious favors of fortune." But publicly, one pays "a superior deference to the great lord above the vassal, because riches are the most convenient, being the most fixed and determinate source of distinction."[7] Riches are a "convenient" and "determinate" criterion because they are what enable a man to be virtuous — to please and to be useful — as a man without riches almost never can be.

In this, if in little else, Hume and Dr. Johnson agree. The latter is emphatic on money's being prior to personal merit — prior instrumentally, not ontologically. "Go into the street," he says, "and give one man a lecture on morality, and another a shilling, and see which will respect you most." Those who argue for the advantages of poverty, as he himself did when he was young, are found to be very sorry to be poor. A large income, rightly spent, can bring happiness; a small income is likely to keep happiness from coming at all:

> Poverty takes away so many means of doing good, and produces so much inability to resist evil, both natural and moral, that it is by all virtuous means to be avoided. Consider a man whose fortune is very narrow; whatever be his rank by birth, or whatever his reputation by intellectual excellence, what good can he do? or what evil can he pre-

vent? That he cannot help the needy is evident; he has nothing to spare. But, perhaps, his advice or admonition may be useful. His poverty will destory his influence: many more can find that he is poor, than that he is wise; and few will reverence the understanding that is of so little advantage to its owner.[8]

That is precisely Butler's contention. Money is nothing in itself, it is useful only when we part with it. Like the words of our language, coins are the outward signs of "an inward and spiritual purchasing power" which is realized when they are exchanged.[9] And what we exchange them for are the necessaries of food, clothing, shelter, etc. which ensure our material comfort, that we may go on to learn amiability, to exercise our genius, or to gain whatever reputation we desire. Since we can't cultivate any of these if we are materially pinched, Butler concludes that no loss can be as serious as the loss of money — money, again, being the covenanted sign of our ability to buy the material goods we can't do without.

We can summon more courage against terminal illness or the death of our loved ones than we can against financial ruin. In the first instance, as long as we have money to pay for a warm bed and a nurse, we will die quietly enough, living life to the dregs no matter what the pain. In the second instance, we are like Job, who "probably felt the loss of his flocks and herds more than that of his wife and family — for he could enjoy his flocks and herds without his family, but not his family — not for long — if he had lost all his money." Loss of money can prevent us from maintaining or repairing our health; it can turn friends and family against us in anger, when they discover that we are no sure stay after all, but "have been obtaining esteem under false pretences." After loss of money comes loss of health, then loss of reputation — the latter being, in spite of Cassio, a bad third, since it is usually based on violations of "parvenues conventions," not on violations of the established canons of material and carnal well-being. With health and money, we can live happy "without any reputation at all." But suppose, out of a desire to exert our reputation for others' good, we grow a new one, "as a lobster grows a new claw": what chance (to echo Dr. Johnson) does our new reputation have to influence them if we are poor, and they see how little material good it has done us?

It is hard to deny the cogency of this, once we realize that Butler is arguing not for money's ontological value — it has none — but for its instrumental value. Job's "flocks and herds" are instruments for obtaining the tokens with which he can obtain a mule for his wife and a doctor for himself. These things secured, he will be free to study God's mighty works, and to worship. Job's more-than-material ends were, in a different theological key, Butler's also. That is why he made it a point of honor to be wealthy — to be set up in a way which allowed him to pursue his moral and aesthetic campaigns, whether in the reading room of the British Museum or in the nooks along the coast of Sicily. Like Darwin, Hume, and Dr. Johnson, Butler turned the truism "We need material goods" into a truth, and gave it a grounding in which his precursors' interests in natural science, associational psychology, and social ethics overlap.

He was least percipient about the branch of the latter called political economy, but even there he was so refreshingly candid and unapologetic that, as E. M. Forster says, no one who read him could afterwards ignore the importance of money, or pretend it was vulgar.[10] It is from Butler that Shaw, for instance, learned to be unhypocritical about a good life's requiring money. In his "Preface" to *Major Barbara* he honors Froissart's knight for claiming "a good life" as his birthright, and for being honest enough to say that the way to get it was "to rob and pill." The problem with medieval society was that robbing and pilling actually did lead to "a good life," when they should have led to the gallows. If modern society were properly organized, those who quietly robbed and pilled (i.e., lived on what are called independent incomes) *would* go to the gallows — or as Shaw aseptically puts it, "to the lethal chamber."

> But as [he continues], thanks to our political imbecility and personal cowardice (fruits of poverty, both), the best imitation of a good life now procurable is life on an independent income, all sensible people aim at securing such an income, and are, of course, careful to legalize and moralize both it and all the actions and sentiments which lead to it and support it as an institution. What else can they do? They know, of course, that they are rich because others are poor. But they cannot help that: it is for the poor to repudiate poverty when they have had enough of it.[11]

The passage makes one think of Margaret Schlegel in *Howards End*, self-consciously clipping her coupons and cashing them in on concerts, pictures, tours, books, and tea. She sees her money as an island holding her up over the flood of the "unthinkable" poor; she shocks Mr. Wilcox by specifying the size of her island, and by expecting him to specify the size of his. She is in effect Alethaea Pontifex's progressively modified descendant, the intelligent woman for whom Shaw wrote his guide to socialism and capitalism. She doesn't pretend that she can live without her island, and, wanting others to have islands just as beautifully furnished, she vaguely feels that they will get them as soon as they want them badly enough. And the sooner the better, since the abundance of life on one island finally depends on that throughout the whole archipelago.

Once more we have seen Butler as a mediator between the assumptions of his created precursors and those of his heirs. In economics he advances the wisdom of the former either by expressing it more wittily, or by interpreting it according to Victorian conditions, or by eluding the Mammon-worshipper's trap of supposing that material realities are the only realities. In turn, his heirs advance his ideal of the moneyed life to the point where it applies explicitly to everyone — an egalitarian dream the realization of which he himself would believe more distant than even the Fabian Shaw predicts, but the importance of which he would salute because it *is* a dream, an attempt to subvert the Malthusian equations. What his heirs conceive in economics is in principle not alien to what he himself says about the importance of money: they simply take him at his word and look for ways to get everyone well set up. The distance between Butler and his heirs is therefore not intellectual; it is emotional. Neither Shaw nor Forster ever confuses economic and sexual struggle, but Butler does, and to such a degree as to disable some critics from taking seriously anything he writes on either head. It is here that the branches of the Butlerian bivium sadly collapse into one another.

After Ernest has come into his inheritance, he returns to Battersby to see his dying mother. Theobald has heard nothing about the legacy, and has sent a check for the train fare and for a suit of clothes. Ernest is dandied up — as finely as "Towneley himself." Theobald stands aghast and Ernest "put out his hand and said laughingly, 'Oh it's all paid for — I am afraid you do not know that Mr. Overton has handed over to me Aunt Alethaea's money.' Theobald flushed scarlet ..." and so on (*WAF,* 321f). It is obvious that Butler is using his novel to over-indulge his wish to revenge himself against his father for the years of financial insecurity which a bit of generosity and a more obligingly early death might have relieved. But there is worse behind. Having failed to assert himself sexually against his father, whether by literally usurping his mother's affection or by transferring the struggle to another relationship, Ernest quarrels with him on economic grounds, where "Oh, it's all paid for" shouts defiance.[12] All vital, erotic pugnacity is missing — and no doubt because Theobald is himself such a sexual nonentity that he doesn't in the least call Ernest out. Their quarrel *has* to be economic, since there isn't enough emotional energy to fuel any other kind. Even the ethico-theological quarrel, of which Butler has made a great deal, seems at the moment of Ernest's return to Battersby to have been subsumed under the economic quarrel — as though his new ideas about divinity needed to be reified "in grey Ulster and blue and white necktie." The scene is a facer for anyone who respects Butler: the man could evidently be extraordinarily petty. But was he also self-deluded? Did he think Ernest's appearance, and the sharp words which turn his father an ashen color, amount to a happy coming of age?[13] At one level, yes: the teller of the tale was no doubt smugly conscious of having "won" against his father. But as Lawrence says, we don't want to trust the teller, for he doesn't necessarily know what he has told. Trust the tale instead. At that level, where the teller's unconscious has been busy, a truer sort of knowledge resides, just as Butler insisted from *Erewhon* on. At that level, he may be said to understand his occasional pettiness, affectional exhaustion, and confusion of Eros and Mammon, and to understand with an immediacy which his urbanity only half-hides. His unconscious gives him away, just as Ernest's has given him away in the Miss Maitland episode, by pushing him into a desperate attempt to grasp the object of his desire, wherein he may triumph, but will more likely discover both the inadequacy of the object and the awkwardness with which he is reaching for it. What Butler does after his unconscious has pushed him into that sort of position is the subject of my final chapter.

6

"The Pig Tribe" and the Life of the Mind

While the Victorians who survived into the Edwardian age were horrified at Butler's rebelliousness, many post-Edwardians have complained that he wasn't rebellious enough. Though he attacked the Victorian ecclesiastical, educational, and scientific establishments with some success, though he gave what looked like the coup de grace to the God-fearing Victorian family, he didn't promulgate the overthrow of capitalism or the disestablishment of the Church, nor in his personal life was he the hirsute Bohemian, the uncloseted pederast, or the Byronic libertine which some readers believe his hedonism should have made him. To the disaffected modern, he seems, in short, too like the complacent Victorians he was supposed to undo: rather than plant explosives at Greenwich Observatory, he potted geraniums at Clifford's Inn. My final task is to reach a fair judgment of what the Butlerian rebellion is — to understand why he went as far as he did, and whether he was justified in stopping.

I

The Butlerian canon is replete with apologies for what his enemies would call systematic complacency. Anyone who builds his house upon conscious ideas, he writes in *Life and Habit,* is building upon the sand. One must build instead upon the unconscious ideas of the day — "the current cant and practice of one's peers" — for over the millennia those ideas have hardened into a "rock which, though not immovable — and itself formerly a quicksand — is still most hard to move" (57). Every idea was once new, and many who adopted it were sucked under in the attempt to make it solve the problems posed by invaders, by disease, or by changes in natural and social climate. But when the quicksand of conscious ideas turns into the rock of unconscious ones — when, i.e., they become habits — then the house upon them is nothing less than a fortified tenement. Men are redoubtable when they move in a pack, and their leader is he who sees just so far ahead that they too will see when he shows them, but not so far that they will be puzzled (*WAF*, 18). George Pontifex is a leader in this sense, with enough foresight to make a killing in the religious book trade, but not enough to go in for the anti-religious, which in pre-Victorian England would have bankrupted him. Ernest's parents, in turn, are members of the pack: that is their strength and their justification. If Theobald is a nastier father than his neighbors, it isn't by much: "... in those days fathers were always thrashing their boys." The morality of thrashing is determined not by the consequences for the thrasher and the thrashed, but simply by the pack-rule which enjoins thrashing: "At that time it was universally admitted that to spare the rod was to spoil the child, and St. Paul had placed disobedience to parents in very ugly company" (21) — namely, sodomy, fornication, covetousness, maliciousness, murder, etc. (Romans 1:28–30). We may protest when Theobald performs his Pauline duty by reddening his hand against the tot who he thinks *won't* produce "come" instead of "tum," but he is secure in following the example of "the majority of sensible well-to-do people[,]...[the] *par excellence* guardians and teachers of truth" (245).

The dynamics inside the Pontifex family are continuous with those outside. A leader like Dean Alford sees far enough in the New Testament to put together a commentary which makes a show of disinterested inquiry, but not so far as actually to be disinterested. He simply massages the clerical brain, alerting it to the discrepancies between the accounts of the resurrection, then asking it to take the miracle on faith. He doesn't see what Ernest readily sees because he doesn't *want* to. He is therefore a sort of liar, but no matter: he is also eminently successful and admired by his countrymen, just as the apes who stayed in the trees and got plenty to eat were eminent in their day, though some few of their brothers, sensing the inevitable depletion of the arboreal food supply, were trying their skill on the ground by venturing out onto the savannahs. But if one puts it that way, the issue of "success" is obviously queered: short-term success may mean long-term failure. More confounding, short-term success may involve practices which are in themselves repulsive: would we approve of "cannibalism or infanticide, or even habitual untruthful-

ness of mind," however much these were underwritten by the news-
papers and the colleges? This conundrum, which Ernest works
through for himself along lines strikingly parallel to those drawn in
On Liberty, is clearly identical with that which confronts us among
the Erewhonian eugenicists. The goddess Ydgrun, the voice of the
"sensible well-to-do," may approve of the elimination of the sick and
the stunted, but we don't. The upshot is that the rock upon which our
Ydgrunite tenement is built "is not infallible": the occasional
foolishness or hideousness of majority sentiment reveals the
quicksand it once was, and leaves us dependent on our instinct to
guide us along routes where our neighbors do not go — routes over
which we haven't been ourselves, but which we have faith will prove
traversable.

Butler nears the end of these meditations, which I have been both
summarizing and extending, with the wink of a geometer who has
been tracing a line with a compass, pushing out the pencil-end just
enough to describe an enlarging spiral instead of a closed circle:
"And so my hero returned *almost* to the point from which he had
started originally, namely that the just shall live by faith" (my italics).
That final clause is a Pauline formula for an un-Pauline religionist.
Ernest won't put his faith "in the supernatural element of the Christian religion," and he naively expects that the Archbishop of Canterbury soon won't either. If he can only get the Archbishop to take a
hard look at Dean Alford on the bridge, he will join him (Ernest) in
the lifeboat. As a warm up, Ernest tries to do for the prison chaplain
what Mr. Shaw the tinker has done for him, but with indifferent
results: "I do not suppose he believed in the actual objective truth of
the stories about Christ's resurrection and ascension more than
Ernest did, but he knew that this was a small matter, and that [the]
real issue lay much deeper than this" (245–48). Instead of telling
Ernest what the "real issue" is, the chaplain prefers to fuss over
practical matters such as what he will do when he leaves prison — a
change of conversational direction which, maddeningly, Butler
pursues as well. What is the "deeper" business which, if it can't
justify Dean Alford's New Testament commentary, can at least justify
the maintenance of the established Church as a witness to things not
seen?

The answer for Ernest comes in two stages. First, he must endeavor
to realize for himself the goal of all religious life, the devout, gentle-
manly wish "to get on comfortably in the world, and to look, and be,
as nice as possible." Emulating Towneley is his way of adopting the

cant and practice of his peers — or rather, his way of indicating *which* of his peers he reverences most. For his epoch is hardly unanimous in what it considers to be the ideal of human development, and at Cambridge he is caught between the models posed by the Simeonites and "the best set" — the Badcocks and the goodcocks — a polarity he faces in subtler form in London when he has to contrast Towneley and the speciously civilized Pryer. His choice is viscerally determined: "The faces of men [like Towneley]...were open and kindly; they looked as if at ease themselves and as though they would set all who had to do with them at ease as far as might be. The faces of Pryer and his friends were not like this" (221–22). As we have seen, though, Ernest's desire to be "the perfect gentleman" is finally doomed: he hasn't the innate physiological advantages Towneley's ancestors bequeathed him, nor the domestic advantages Towneley's parents rendered him by dying when he was an infant and leaving him heir to one of the richest estates in England.[1] While for Towneley belief in the Church of England is "a matter of course," an exercise in Laodiceanism, for Ernest nothing is "a matter of course." Whether in belief, in unbelief, or in agnosticism, he is incurably earnest — serious, probing, introspective, academic.

Ernest is one of the numerous Victorians for whom the Schillerian epigraph to *Past and Present* — "*Ernst ist das Leben*" — is not simply a curse; it is a one-line vade mecum. Because Ernest is earnest, he can realize the deeper issue of religion in a second way. If Towneley is the consummate heir, living with unconscious grace, Ernest is the aspiring pioneer, living by conscious principles. The one roosts on solid rock, the cynosure of "the best set." The other is never more than a hanger-on of such people, and he finally lets himself slide off the rock altogether in order to tread the quicksand. His hope is that he himself can press some of the sand into new rock, and that his own heirs will complete the job, adding stratum to stratum till they stand on a butte which Towneley's heirs, startled at last into self-consciousness, will have to gaze up at. This is the dimly conceived substance of Ernest's "faith in his own destiny," his believing, "Rightly or wrongly,...[that] he possessed a strength which if he were only free to use it in his own way might do great things some day" (254). Awkward and principled people like him once made possible "the most fortunate kind of modern European"; now he may help to make possible a kind "still more fortunate" (*LH*, 30). His labor naturally complements Butler's. He writes books on divorce and inheritance laws, on child-rearing, and on theological controversy, variously trying to remove whatever would obstruct the body-soul in its activity, so that generations immediately following his own needn't suppose that the idea of the holy depends on a belief in the bodily resurrection of Christ, that the education of children depends on corporal punishment, or that the livelihood of adults depends on the fiscal good will of parents bent on becoming octogenarians. It is hard to be very particular about what the lives of Ernest's descendants will look like. Butler is clear about immediate demolition projects, and is willing to fantasy a post-ice age people who will learn to read and sum with the facility we now show in learning to walk and talk. The time between tomorrow and the schoolmarm's millennium, however, he leaves indeterminate; it is for other generations to direct their lives according to their own lights. Their freedom to do so is what Ernest's quiet pioneering is meant to guarantee.

The tension between the need to accommodate oneself to the cant and practice of one's peers and the need to pioneer toward that of the future may be traced back to Precambrian times, when there occurred "the first great schism or heresy... in what was heretofore the catholic faith of protoplasm," the sundering of plants and animals. The one sect thought it better to stay home and profit from what came along, while the other decided to go in search of prey.[2] Different species within either sect still have to make similar decisions — a plant asking whether it ought to stay put or to impinge, say, upon higher ground, where there is more sun but earlier frost; and an animal asking whether it should graze the river banks only, or risk going onto the plain. There are, in short, animal ways of being a plant, and vegetal ways of being an animal.

Ernest's choices may be seen accordingly. His yearning to be like Towneley is vegetal: he wants to root himself in a prescribed routine of dressing à la Bond Street, taking country walks on Sundays, vacationing where the climate is warm and the people are handsome, and preferring the easy laughter of the pantomime to the violent catharsis of the tragic drama. His coming to rest in quiet enjoyment is like *À la recherche du temps perdu* written backwards — not the recovery, but the discovery of pleasure:

> ...the fireplace with a fire in it, the easy chairs, the Times, my cat, the red geraniums in my window, to say nothing of coffee, bread and butter, sausages, marmalade, etc. Everying [Overton says] was pregnant with the most exquisite pleas-

> ure to him. The plane trees were full of leaf still; he kept
> rising from the breakfast table to admire them; never till
> now, he said, had he known what the enjoyment of these
> things really was. (WAF, 266)

Rewarding as this Combreyesque enjoyment is for Ernest, it is
adequate neither to his nervous sytem nor to his intellectual genius.
For he has the un-Towneley impulse to be animal: he wants to
wander out of all prescribed routines, to be solitary like Ishmael,
more at home upon desert sand than on Pall Mall cobblestone. There
is, of course, a negative side to his animality. While on one hand he
isn't fit to be a thriving plant, on the other the animals he is supposed
to imitate — "the hippopotamus, the rhinoceros, . . . the elephants . . .
and the pig tribe generally" (307, my italics) — however vicious
when threatened, are as a rule sedentary if not wallowing. While
Towneley may be said to resemble a fine Morgan stud now out to
pasture, Ernest resembles a wild boar whose tusks are used more for
rooting than for goring. But his animality does have its positive side:
the wild boar will charge if provoked, it will risk its life if sufficient
cause be given. Which is to say, Ernest will as a last resort push away
his neighbors and his family and, in very desperation, think and feel
for himself.

But how is he to know when the "last resort" is called for? If in the
natural course of things his greatest comfort would be to have his
neighbors' and his family's approbation, how shall he know himself
justified in risking their disapprobation, and the loss of his smaller
material comforts besides? He shall know at the moment he feels his
essential self — those qualities which define him and not someone
else — stultified or swallowed by another. We have watched how this
happens with regard to theology and sexuality. In both those cases
Christina assumes the role of seductress, persuading him, as Thomas
Arnold would have, that apropos of "the difficulties of a clergyman's
position" he knows "all" he needs to, despite the fact that she hasn't
told him what the difficulties are (184); and that, apropos of who got
Ellen pregnant, he could've if he would've, but thanks to his pure
upbringing, he wouldn't. She uses him, in the one case, to make
herself piously soporific, and in the other, to give herself a mild
titillation: she defines a double-Ernest to feed her own contradictions, "a kind of Joseph and Don Juan in one" (159). The threat which
we haven't yet considered carefully, however, is directed against his
aesthetic sensibility. It is his response to this which brings us to

realize that, for him, the one thing needful is finally not his neighbors' approbation, or his family's, but his own.

II

When Ernest goes up to Cambridge he reads a great deal, not indeed because he associates reading with pleasure, but because the dons and his fellow undergraduates tell him he should: "...his natural instinct, like that of all very young men who are good for anything, was to do as those in authority told him" (173). It is not long, however, before he discovers that the authorities can't always be trusted. To begin with, his reading doesn't necessarily feel like the duty they say it is; as long as the right book is in his hands, it can feel like a pleasure. And more, the right book usually isn't the one the authorities recommend.

> ...[W]hich of us *in his heart* likes any of the Elizabethan dramatists except Shakespeare [Ernest writes]? Are they in reality anything else than literary Struldbrugs?
> ...Aristophanes did not like any of the tragedians ... they were a fraud, or something very like it. For my own part I *cordially* agree with him. I am *free to confess* that with the exception, perhaps, of some of the psalms of David I know no writings which seem so little to deserve their reputation. (177, my italics)

Ernest has moved from mechanical obedience to free discrimination. He probably couldn't reach the latter activity without beginning in the former — someone must put him in the way of books before he can learn which, if any, are good for him. But how disastrous it would be if he always did as he was told. Disobedience is what distinguishes a human reader from a television camera, and the words or phrases I have italicized in the above passage are hardly throw-aways: they emphasize the importance of the visceral, the spontaneous, the affective dimension of right reading. The burden of proof lies with those who say a book is good, when Ernest himself so "cordially" dislikes it *as* he reads.

One is reminded of Mark Twain's Philistine but candid definition of a classic: a book which everyone wishes to say he has read, but which no one wishes to read. And one suspects that Butler's acquaintance with the legion of what he thought were "literary Struldbrugs" — Plato, Euripides, Dante, Goethe, Dickens, etc. — was pretty superficial. As Shaw scoldingly puts it:

> He "hated"...everyone who did not appeal to his palate
> instantly as a lollypop appeals to the palate of a child.... [I]t
> is plain that Butler did seriously narrow his mind and
> paralyse his critical powers by refusing to take any trouble to
> find out what our greatest teachers were driving at, or to face
> the drudgery of learning their peculiar idiom.... It is really
> appalling to learn that this man of genius, having received
> the very best education our most expensive and select in-
> stitutions could give him, and having withal a strong natural
> taste for music and literature, turned from Bayreuth in mere
> ignorant contempt, and yet made every Christmas a pious
> pilgrimage to the Surrey pantomime, and wrote an anx-
> iously careful account of its crude buffooneries to his musi-
> cian friend.[3]

Granting all this, I think we must also grant the central truth of
Butler's insistence that a work of art "appeal to his palate" — if not
"instantly," then at least in good time. What, after all, would Shaw's
heroes, Wagner and Ibsen, have accomplished had they deceived
themselves about Rossini's or Scribe's effect on their palates? What
indeed would Shaw himself have accomplished had he not spat out
the economic and theatric assumptions of, say, Jerrold's *The Rent-
Day* or Mrs. Wood's *East Lynne*? Though unconsciously an artist
might retain many assumptions of the past, palatable and unpalatable both, he must consciously imagine himself as eschewing the
bulk of them, else, daunted by what "they" have done, he will do
nothing himself. What Harold Bloom has called the anxiety of
influence is something Butler dealt with instinctively: the best way
to handle influences is to show them the door! Nothing can remove
the necessity for first-hand and even naive approaches to problems
in the arts or in philosophy. A Raphael or a Bishop Berkeley may
already have reached a solution to a particular problem, or have got
to the point where, the problem being fully articulated, it is obvious
no solutions are forthcoming, but in either case we won't truly
understand till we have gone through their movements ourselves.
We may wish to summarize as many of their first steps as possible,
though we should do so cautiously, without assuming too much. But
we *must* try the problem from scratch — wherever we decide
"scratch" is — if we expect either to know what they knew, or to

know more. And whether we end up knowing more or not, the pursuit will reward us handsomely if we honestly enjoy it — if, that is, we are happy in it when we are by ourselves and nobody is watching. Butler asks us whether we would study a painting if we were absolutely alone, or would paint one if we knew that only ourselves and a few intimate friends would ever see it. Likewise with music, literature, philosophy, and science: none of these has a sake of its own, for only people can have a sake.

It does often seem that a writer, for example, has written for others' sakes, but that is so only because he first wrote for his own. Let my art be for my sake, Butler says; let us have a periodical written and illustrated entirely by amateurs

> who look and think for themselves, and express themselves just as they please....Every contributor should be at once turned out if he or she is generally believed to have tried to do something which he or she did not care about trying to do, and anything should be admitted which is the outcome of a genuine liking. People are always good company when they are doing what they really enjoy.[4]

There could not have been anything as national as Bayreuth till Wagner had devoted himself to the harmonics and the mythology he personally liked. Not that those harmonics or that mythology were wholly sui generis, but that they must to some degree have seemed so to Wagner when he was composing. He who self-consciously imitates, and no more, produces banality all round, for himself as well as for his audience. What looks like deliberate imitation in Butler is often a subterfuge for securing ends private to himself. He takes the sacrament once a year, composes his oratorio "Narcissus" in the Handelian manner, and lets The Way of All Flesh run on in a Trollopean vein largely for the purpose of keeping the peace with his neighbors. It is a means of accommodation via prevarication, feigning, like the lapwing, so as to ensure the liberty to do what he more essentially wants: to keep in touch, through the sacrament, with the larger truth that there is an invisible power in the universe, and to keep at bay the larger falsehood that all reality is compassed by the claims of materialistic science; to write a farce, through the oratorio, upon the weal and woe of capitalism; and through the loose baggy monster, to conflate allegory, treatise, commonplace book, denunciation of anathema, and writ of indulgence.

It is curious that Ernest is at Cambridge when he learns that he must read and write for his own sake: one would think he would need to get away from there altogether before he could learn something so valuable. But perhaps, by accident, the ancient university does sometimes foster genuine work by presenting the great artists and philosophers in a manner so dull that an inquiring undergraduate, if he manages to continue to think at all, will assume that they are dullards, and go on to tackle problems afresh on his own. As a rule, however, Cambridge, like Oxford and the public schools, fosters mediocrity by centering her instruction in what the Erewhonian Colleges of Unreason call "hypothetics" — the useless and tedious materials that go toward the classical and mathematical tripos. That is why the focus of the Butlerian education — Muggeridge says he was a don, though "at a one-man university" — is reality: that which is useful and pleasant, that which encourages a student to attend to subjects because they will make his schoolyears, and his later ones, richer than Butler's own had been. We have seen how the traditional public school subjects are attended with lots of corporal punishment and mental drudgery, "but no good comfortable bribes." Growing bone and muscle, on the contrary, is useful and pleasant both, for one does it by eating good food, playing games, and performing the right amount of physical labor. Ernest always masters what is useful or pleasant to him, and always forgets what isn't. When he is leaving Roughborough, he is given a little volume off Dr. Skinner's shelf:

> The book was one written in Latin by a German — Schömann, 'De comitiis Atheniensibus' — not exactly light and cheerful reading, but Ernest felt it was high time he got to understand the Athenian constitution and manner of voting; he had got them up a great many times already, but had forgotten them as fast as he had learned them...How strange it was: he wanted to remember these things very badly [or so the voice of Theobald tells him]; he knew he did, but he could never retain them... [w]hereas if anyone played him a piece of music and told him where it came from, he never forgot that, though he made no effort to retain it, and was not even conscious of trying to remember it at all. His mind must be badly formed and he was no good. (170)

It is all a question of *wanting* to learn, in the sense both of needing and of desiring. When Ernest is training as a tailor in prison, the people in authority praise his work — something no teacher has ever done for him — and he improves as much in three months as many men do in twelve. When he is dealing in used clothes with Ellen, he quickly becomes a fair hand: "Knowledge of this sort is very easily acquired by anyone who is in *bona fide* want of it" (282). People who learn to ride a bicycle never forget how: they have enjoyed it, they have got places faster on it than they could on foot, they have acquired a habit. That sort of learning, Ernest discovers, doesn't come from his classes with the switch-bearers; it comes from his off-hours sessions with the organist at St. Michael's, from his runs in the fields around Battersby, from his conversations with well-met strangers, and most of all, from his Odysseyan journey through the dingy, necessitous world of Ashpit Place, prison, and tailordom.

Suppose that everyone were given the ideal Butlerian education, impelled by utility and by pleasure. We would get a society where all are perfectly accommodated to all, where disputes either are unheard of or are settled amicably out of court, and where all movements necessary for survival are made instinctively. Butler envisages a society which will consummate our current efforts of legislative and mechanical invention in an "unconscious state of equilibrium" among men, and between men and their tools, analogous to the equilibrium

> we observe in the structures and instincts of bees and ants, and an approach to which may be found among some savage nations. We may reflect, however, not without pleasure, that this condition — the true millennium — is still distant. Nevertheless the ants and bees seem happy; perhaps more happy than when so many social questions were in as hot discusssion among them, as other, and not dissimilar ones, will one day be amongst ourselves. (*LH*, 162)

I know of no other passage in Butler which so closely encapsulates his ambivalence about his own purpose in life. To attain the "happy" millennium of the ant heap, the amalgamated citizens, each as nice and as insouciantly efficient as Towneley himself, living gracefully even through fire and flood with the automatic responses all the ant-ages past have bequeathed them — Butler has pricked us toward this peculiar city of God by crying up "the race for unconsciousness" (30). And on the other hand he reflects, "not without pleasure," that

the race will be very long in running, for is there not a satisfaction —
as large as, if not larger than that to be had in the milennium — in the
running itself? Surely the millennium will obviate the favorite
activity of Butler's career, the tearing down of the obstacles between
our present cacaphony and our future unison. In principle he is even
now incorporate with all others of his species, and only the imperfections of political and educational machinery prevent them from
advancing together. But, to repeat the calm remark which echoes
more truly as a shout in all of Butler, "We want to be ourselves; we do
not want any one else to claim part and parcel of our identity. This
community of identities is not found to answer in everyday life" (80).
Like Dostoevsky's Underground Man, Butler would rather kick the
ant heap over than live in it.

Or if, by virtue of his membership in a species which he can't
dissolve, he is compelled to take part in the race for unconsciousness, he insists on the role of coach. We look again on the River Cam
during Butler's time up, when he coxed for a boat of Johannian
athletes, feeding them their ideas, training them till they could
execute them blindfolded and row beyond the mark — they oblivi-
ous of their puissance, he admiring what he had wrought. Some of
his disparagers have of course sneered that his admiration is mostly
voyeuristic — the puny cox leering at the thin-clad oarsmen, and so
on. Without denying the presence of such a mood in Butler, I would
submit first that his admiration is more for how their capacities can
develop under the guidance of his own cunning, and second that it is
mixed not just with envy — one naturally wants to row as well as to
cox — but with contempt. Contempt for the Towneleys? That sounds
doubtful, but only till we remember Towneley's original, the
blackguardly and yet handsome Charles Paine Pauli, with whom
Butler could never break, but toward whom he must early on have
felt little attachment, so uninterested was the fellow in any of the
aesthetic or philosophic passions which governed the major part of
his life. The mode of his entire career as a writer presupposes such a
valuation, the knowledge that he was different in kind from the
Barbarians who, as Arnold said, were incapable of thought. And
though he would have shuddered at the proposal that he belong to
any group, he was in effect a member of Arnold's cultural elite — the
intelligentsia who do the conscious work which he eloquently
honored Nausicaa, Shakespeare, Handel, and Lamarck for doing.
And he honored them more sensibly than Shaw was finally to honor
his particular heroes, for he never made the mistake of *Back to*

Methuselah, which fancies them as precursors to a millennium of pure consciousness, somehow divorced, in the whirl of the "vortex," from all matter. Life is the conjunction of spirit and matter: consciousness disembodied is not a higher stage, it is nothing.

III

Applying Thomas Mann's distinction between the sons of nature (Goethe and Tolstoy) and the sons of spirit (Schiller and Dostoevsky), one knows that Butler belongs with the latter. His over-praise of the "natural" Italian peasants, of his "natural" Cockney manservant Alfred, and of the "natural" Barbarian swells is only what Mann identifies as the son of spirit's envy of his own opposite, an envy which is but the jaundiced obverse of a more essential feeling of superiority. The knack for being acutely conscious of the puzzle of his own and any thing's existence is a troubled blessing for Butler. Indeed he so often regards consciousness as a plague that many critics have pictured him as a writer who ultimately died of self-loathing. But in fact his purpose was less to loathe his consciousness than to moderate and guide it in beneficent directions.

It is Ernest's inheritance of hyperactive consciousness which renders him susceptible to Simeonism. At the very moment he is sophomorically exhorting the Sims "to a freer use of the tub," he is getting ready to try to emulate these same throwbacks to the primitive Christians who, as Paul says, were "neither well-bred nor intellectual people," and who "gloried in the fact that in the flesh they had not much to glory" (183). This sounds ominous, yet for a fellow born clever but not sensible, it is an indispensible step toward a life more advantageous to the flowering of his genius. The sensible parishoners back at Battersby would have been as appalled to see Christianity doubted as to see it practiced. Ernest *must* either doubt or practice, and he can do neither honestly without giving the other a good go. "I am now going towards Christ; the greater number of my college friends are, I fear, going away from him..." (198). This is such a good go that Theobald is frightened out of his wits. Though himself more low Church than high, he is willing to let himself rise with the tide effected by the Oxford Movement, and here Ernest is threatening to dive into evangelicalism.

He is being foolish all right, sowing what are in fact "an exceedingly tame and uninteresting crop" of spiritual wild oats among the hard-up and unchurchly denizens of Ashpit Place. Yet it is his very willingness to go against the grain, to dart like a snipe in a direction

which neither "the good men" at Cambridge nor his own devout
parents approve of, that guarantees his arrival at a new and richer
stage of development. Theobald never grows out of the Church
because he hasn't the courage to enter, in all seriousness, into it.
Ernest has the foolish courage to enter in, and he dies in action — or
rather, like an embryo, he suffers "a pro tanto death" as one phase
metamorphoses into another, the Battersby Christian giving way to
the "Hawke-ish" Christian, who in turn gives way to the excited
unbeliever, who in turn gives way to the Broad Churchman still
earnest enough to evangelize. And evangelize not in renewed belief
that the cow jumped over the moon, but in surety that, while the
spirit of the Church is true though her letter is true no longer, the
spirit of "the Huxleys and Tyndalls is as lying as its letter" (334).
Ernest's outward devotion may look as unexceptionably Laodicean
as Towneley's, but it is qualitatively different, not just because he has
arrived at it through earnest practice and doubt, according to the best
soul-saving and mind-saving counsels of his day, but because he
grasps his pen more readily than his opium pipe. He is a combative
religionist who no longer rings people's doorbells.

Butler is evangelizing on behalf of the mind — the whole of our
mental activity which he usually designates by the word "spirit," but
which doesn't exclude what we ordinarily call "reason." The final
paragraph of Life and Habit so impresses readers that they are prone
to suppose that Butler is primarily a poet or mystic who, like Blake,
wants to overthrow the tyrant Urizen ("y'r-reason").

> Will the reader bid me wake with him to a world of chance
> and blindness? Or can I persuade him to dream with me of a
> more living faith than either he or I had as yet conceived as
> possible? As I have said, reason points remorselessly to an
> awakening, but faith and hope still beckon to the dream.
> (250)

"Reason" is a straw-man easy to knock down for immediate rhetori-
cal purposes. But if we follow Life and Habit attentively, we will see
that reason is allied to believing, hoping, "dreaming": it is the
instrument, they are the motive power, all functioning together as
parts of the intelligent will which enables organisms to adapt themselves to the exigencies of their milieux. Darwin's great blasphemy,
according to Butler, was to employ his own reason in the cause of
picturing a universe in which reason had no part — the spiritual

self-impalement of forwarding the theory of circumstantial selection, wherein the creaturely and rational choice of means and ends is
said not to count. Butler gave the lie to that theory not just by writing
his philippics against Darwinism, but by being the dreaming-
reasoning man of will he was. What he *was* may at times have
seemed to him a calamity: "Above all things, let no unwary reader do
me the injustice of believing in *me*. In that I write at all I am among
the damned" (*LH*, 35). But each time he wrote a sentence he must
have seen himself as more truly among the anointed — a chrysalis
wet with promise. He knew his damnation was only for the time
being — a bother of ill-fitting clothes, wrinkled mien, tottering
accounts, and a heart that was an echo-chamber. But these discomforts weren't infernal. They were at worst purgatorial, the temporary
sufferings of a creature who, if he exercised his powers of mind
aright, would metamorphose into something blessedly different. He
could look forward to a life to come, whereas those who for the time
being were happy in their clothes, mien, accounts, and heart would
in all likelihood know nothing thereafter better than the privilege of
enriching the loam they would lie under.

Butler's life to come rested in the memory others would have of
him after his body died. Like the eighteenth-century philosophers,
he believed in what Carl Becker has called the religion of posterity,
according to which this present life is just what revealed religion has
in its own way claimed it to be — a period of probation. How we
spend the time being determines how far we shall endure in the time
to come, and whether that time shall be "a heaven of just affection or
a hell of righteous condemnation" in the hearts of our survivors.
Achilles held the same opinion, though while he gave highest place
to warriors, Butler gives it to makers who don't just make decorous
music, like Virgil and Pope, but appeal to us viscerally, like Homer.
We admire them less than we adore:

> I speak of those who draw us ever more towards them from
> youth to age, and to think of whom is to feel at once that we
> are in the hands of those we love, and whom we would most
> wish to resemble. What is the secret of the hold that these
> people have upon us? Is it not that while, conventionally
> speaking, alive, they most merged their lives in, and were in
> fullest communion with those among whom they lived?
> They found their lives in losing them. We never love the

memory of anyone unless we feel that he or she was himself
or herself a lover.[5]

The emphasis on "fullest communion with those among whom they
lived" certainly justifies the immortality of the makers Butler is
willing, for the moment, to say he adores — Homer, Nausicaa,
Shakespeare, Jane Austen. But it would appear to disqualify Butler
himself, inasmuch as he broke communion with the mass of men
among whom he lived. Like Ernest, he hated "not wisely but too
well" (WAF, 356). It is clear from other passages in his work, however,
that Butler doesn't require the great writer to devote himself to his
immediate neighbors, though that is all right in itself; he just required him to devote himself to someone, whether technically alive
or no. Nausicaa loved the storied Odysseus rather more than the
simpering bucks who loitered round her father's house, and Butler
loved her rather more than any woman vivid for him in Piccadilly or
Piora. The great writer's capacity for love, in short, extends to
anyone who is alive either in the flesh or in memory, and the advantage of his greatness resides in his ability to "understand greatness
better in others whether alive or dead, and choose better company
from these, and enjoy and understand that company better when [he
has] chosen it — [and] also [in his ability]... to give pleasure to the
best people and live in the lives of those who are yet unborn" (84).

   The devotion Butler showed toward his dead was indeed remarkable: even after the campaigns against Darwin had been waged and
The Way of All Flesh written, he gave an incalculable amount of time
to memorizing Shakespeare's sonnets, or to poking about the coves
of Sicily and the tiny dim chapels of northern Italy, all that he might
vindicate the peculiar theories he hoped would disinter something
important about artists who, in their time too, had "found their lives
in losing them." Greater love hath no man than this, that he lay down
his life for these. One shouldn't scoff at the "these," as Shaw does.
Butler may have been right about the authoress of The Odyssey and
about Shakespeare,

> But [Shaw asks] who cared, outside the literary fancy? To the
> mass of people whose very souls' salvation depended on
> whether Erewhon and Life and Habit were sound or un-
> sound it mattered not a dump who wrote the Odyssey, or
> whether Shakespear [sic] was 17 or 70 when he wrote the
> sonnets to Mr W. H.[6]

One should instead marvel at the devotedness with which Butler laid down his life. The objects of his devotion may like Don Quixote's sometimes have been ill-chosen, or he may have misperceived their needs, but he nevertheless demonstrated the spirit in which one ought to keep company with "greatness." This, more than the drawn out parricide of his novel, is what affected the lives of the Bloomsburyites who were his immediate posterity.

It is as if he had found the British Museum to be the center of the universe, and had showed them how enjoyable it was to wander there. I am thinking of a passage in *Jacob's Room*:

> There is in the British Museum an enormous mind. Consider that Plato is there cheek by jowl with Aristotle; and Shakespeare with Marlowe. This great mind is hoarded beyond the power of any single mind to possess it. Nevertheless (as they take so long finding one's walking-stick) one can't help thinking how one might come with a notebook, sit at a desk, and read it all through.
>
> ...And there the Elgin Marbles lie, all night long, old Jones's [the watchman's] lantern sometimes recalling Ulysses, or a horse's head; or sometimes a flash of gold, or a mummy's sunk yellow cheek.[7]

Virginia Woolf learned from Butler that one could never get from the reading desk to the shelves of the British Museum by trying to scramble up directly. One got there — or stood a chance of getting there — only by skipping on in one's own amateur way, refusing to step according to the pieties, the earnest professionalism and specialism, of the late Victorian Age. Naturally, she writes elsewhere, Butler's contemporaries "owed him a grudge...as schoolboys set to do their sums in a dreary schoolroom have a grudge against a boy who passes the window with a butterfly net in his hand and nothing to do but enjoy himself."[8] The fields toward which he was skipping, butterfly net in hand, lay most of the year in the British Museum, or during summers, in the dells and mountains of Italy. The schoolroom which immured his contemporaries lay next to the publisher's offices where the salable books were produced after the formulae which the professional establishments — in theology, science, art history, classical scholarship — approved of. Butler dropped his net upon whatever he found useful and pleasant, trying to find out *for himself* what the best that had been thought and said in the world actually was, and thus by indirection to contribute his mite to it as well. This obviously indicates our reasons for remembering his expressly polemical works, but the cases of the elusive satires or of *The Way of All Flesh* are not essentially different: he gave himself to the creating of a world of things, persons, ideas, and emotions which would be independent of his fussy everyday self — turning even what was literally autobiographical into what would be typical. Any fondly remembered writer has performed his work out of such scrupulously *amateur* impulses, but there is an anecdote about Hume which is particularly relevant. In 1776 Boswell, "being too late for Church, ... went to see Mr. David Hume ... [who was] just a dying." Incredulous, and a bit terrified that Hume should look forward to his own annihilation so placidly, Boswell said, "If I were you, I should regret Annihilation. Had I written such an admirable History, I should be sorry to leave it." Hume returned: "I shall leave that history, of which you are pleased to speak so favourably, as perfect as I can."[9]

IV

No author leaves his work entirely perfect, and as I have indicated throughout this study, Butler has left his rather less perfect than many others have left theirs. The imperfections of his work are one with those which marked his life: his spare sympathy with people here and now, his sexual obtuseness, his aborted economic wisdom, his foot-tapping tolerance for institutions like the family which take so long to die their natural deaths, and finally his misconceptions about where his most important work lay — the misconceptions which sent him tilting in defense of Tabachetti and Gaudenzio di Ferrara when he ought to have been rewriting the last third of *The Way of All Flesh*. I have tried to measure the actual depth of these imperfections and to judge the extent to which Butler can answer back, whether in contrition, in helplessness, or in defiance. The ultimate charge against him has to do with the tone of this answering back — this manner of regarding his own strengths and weaknesses.

As one might expect, the late F. R. Leavis puts the charge more formidably than anyone else, and without the snide cuteness with which Muggeridge damaged his own case. Leavis calls *The Way of All Flesh* a "morbidly egotistic, self-ignorant and Pharisaical performance ... Small-minded, blind and odiously complacent, it has been a breeder and re-inforcer of small-mindedness, blindness and odious self-complacency since it was given to the world — in the formative years of the original Bloomsbury."[10] I have tried, in my third chapter, to remove the morbidity from our conception of Butler's egotism, and in my fifth, to qualify our understanding of what his self-ignorance amounted to. But what about odious complacency? Leavis' mordant judgment recalls Basil Willey's more equable remark that the weakness of High Ydgrunitism as practiced by moralists like Chesterfield and Hume lies in their conflation of the good with the respectable. Their concern is less with self-approval (though that obviously counts) than with others' approval. And the "others" are naturally the members of one's social class or, more dearly, one's set.

The mutual admiration among the several fellows of the Clifford's Inn fraternity led to that among the original Bloomsburyites, a line of influence which is not a Leavisian projection, but a matter of history attested to by the Bloomsburyites themselves — Virginia Woolf, Forster, Strachey, Desmond MacCarthy.[11] It is less the particular ideas than the style of the Bloomsburyites which troubles Leavis: their cosiness, their exclusiveness, their economic parasitism, and their alliances with the centers of intellectual power — Cambridge, the *Times*, the publisher's houses, and the surviving great nineteenth-century journals. As soon as one begins to rehearse the Leavisian protest against Bloomsbury, however, one feels how inapropos it is of Butler himself. A Johannian, a snob, a moneyed parasite he was, but who could have been more at enmity with the authorities at Cambridge or with the respected media of his day? The true differences between him and Leavis are, first, that the one, though he had his scare when his stock in the Canada Tanning Extract Company fell to nothing, never really faced penury, while the other faced it for two decades; and second, that the one could write gracefully and with good humor, while the other wrote as Henry James talked, and without a smile. But beyond these differences there is a genuine similarity. Both attended Cambridge and then felt the blight of exclusion from her honored posts; both championed unpopular opinions in defiance of the modish intelligentsia. And most importantly, against the vacuities of that intelligentsia's materialistic science, both defended the imagination's freedom to create according to the numinous power which inspires it. The recurrent Leavisian exemplars of the religious sense — Tom Brangwen's realization, in *The Rainbow*, that he belongs not to himself alone but to the something greater which wheels the stars and helps the ewes to bring forth, and Blake's realization that his poems were his and yet not his, that the poet's imagination draws from the reservoir of a racial imagination — these exemplars could as well have been Butler's. The tenant of Clifford's Inn may have been smug enough, but he was a rigorous combatant, beleaguered too often by his enemies' indifference, yet unceasing in his barrages. Had the equally combative Leavis learned something of Butler's manner, he might have run the risk of being similarly ignored, but certainly not for long, given the vigor of his allies. As it was, his reiterative campaigns went on past even his allies' powers of attention, and many of them, with provocation to be sure, ended up turning on him the kind of dismissive ridicule or nervous indifference which Butler, in his hour, finally triumphed over.

There is, however, another sense in which to understand Leavis' charge of odious complacency, a sense which Willey again approximates in a more equable fashion. He contrasts two kinds of moral error, saying that if virtue is a harmony of inward and outward excellences, then the Puritan errs by so overemphasizing the former, the ideal of intrinsic merit, that he comes to regard it as separable from and even incompatible with outward excellence. The Chesterfieldian, on the other hand, errs by so overemphasizing the outward excellences — "the graces" — that he comes not to scorn intrinsic excellence, which of course he extols, but to neglect it. He simply takes it too much for granted. "Chesterfield's morality," Willey concludes, "is like neo-classicism in art: it cares more for imitation than for depth of life, and values decorum, tact and elegance above the inward energies of which they should be the restraining moulds."[12] Here we have a finger on the potential for moral degradation in Butler's ethical theory. He rightly desired and revered the outward graces, but his admiration for "swells" and "good breeding," however well rationalized in evolutionary terms, and however backed up, one might add, by the contemporary propaganda on behalf of "manliness" put out by writers as different as Thomas Hughes and Leslie Stephen, misled him in the case of Pauli to mistake outward grace for total virtue — the pleasantness of a part with the requisite pleasantness of the whole. But at least in his writing he recognized this danger as well as anyone. I have said enough about the implicitly high valuation which his dedication to letters gave to the cunning life of the mind. There is one more point, though, to be made about his valuation of graceful bodies. *The Way of All Flesh* has as a minor theme the necessity of knowing both outer and inner quality — to distinguish a Towneley, who, with the obvious exception of his nasty sexual practices, is truly nice inside and out, from a speciously handsome Pryer or Hawke, who isn't nice on the inside. Men like Towneley and Badcock are consonant inside and out; it is the confusing signals of a Pryer or Hawke which would give anyone trouble.

Once Ernest has discerned the insinuatingly homosexual and swindling qualities of Pryer and the intellectual dishonesty of Hawke — once, that is, he has found out what's in their names — he is all right. He knows henceforth how to cut anyone or anything similarly bad. But does he cut too much, or too little? And is he harsher toward himself than he need be, or the reverse? These are the questions with which this chapter began, and I won't claim to offer a definitive answer where, in the nature of the case, no such answer can be made. I want simply to picture Butler's best text, *The Way of All Flesh,* in the company of two other *Bildungsromane,* one by Forster and the other by Lawrence. In *The Longest Journey* Forster is suicidally harsh toward himself, for at the end he kills off Rickie Elliot, the young man onto whom he has projected so much of himself. Unable to resolve his story, he can only call upon the railroad train to annihilate the homosexual who can neither cure himself by taking a woman, nor accept himself by taking a man. In Lawrence's *Sons and Lovers* a differently troubled Paul Morel appears to be heading in the same direction as Rickie, but at the end he turns round, his fists clenched, and refuses the way that leads to self-immolation. Butler's novel falls somewhere between these extreme types, and looks perhaps dully serene next to them. Ernest ends up neither in despair nor in administering what Lawrence called tragedy's "great kick at misery."[13] He ends, instead, in self-acceptance. There has been ample reason to despair, his childhood and youth having been quite as wretched as Rickie Elliot's, but he steels himself and resists those who make him wretched — at least enough to win the freedom to muddle on, and sometimes even to dash, without being tripped up by them. Knowing how stunted and unhappy he might have been, he is relieved to be what he is, acquiescing in his friends' sentiment of not wishing him much different, because he knows that "different" is more likely to mean worse than to mean better. The fact that he is what he is may be credited, as we have seen, not just to his circumstantial luck, but to his own unconscious cunning. And as we again have seen, Butler's faith in the latter is something he shares with Lawrence: Ernest's resistance and Paul Morel's are akin. But Paul turns round 180 degrees — the implication being that in his next phase he will be more like Birkin in *Women in Love* than like anything we might expect from Miriam Leivers' boyfriend. Ernest's turn is a slight thirty-some degrees: he cuts his parents, his wife, his children, and his anti-self, but as Overton's crony he is recognizably the descendant of the boy on whom Dr. Skinner fell like a moral landslip, and of the curate who kicked his christening Bible off the table and marched out to accost Miss Maitland. Lawrence's theory of psychological change is naively, bracingly catastrophist: he is like the early geologists who thought the different stages of the earth's history were suddenly made and unmade by violent volcanic and tidal upheaval. Butler's theory is sensibly, quietly, but not resignedly evolutionist: change is possible — we can and must *will* it — but it takes generations to achieve anything radically new. Without Lawrence's sense of the indignity of unhappiness we shall stagnate, but without Butler's sense of the inveteracy of its causes, that indignity is something we shall never be patient and shrewd enough to remove.

Notes

INTRODUCTION

1. Stillman's *Samuel Butler: A Mid-Victorian Modern* (New York: Viking, 1932) remains for every purpose the most thoughtful and comprehensive book on Butler.

2. In his brief "Kafka and His Precursors," Borges culls a number of heterogeneous texts from his reading which he thinks, first, resemble Kafka, and second, do not always resemble each other. "The second fact is the more significant": i.e., *Kafka* gives them their likeness. "The fact is that every writer *creates* his own precursors. His work modifies our conception of the past, as it will modify the future." See *Labyrinths: Selected Stories and Other Writings* (New York: New Directions, 1962), p. 201. The last sentence quoted is of course an allusion to Eliot's "Tradition and the Individual Talent": "The existing monuments form an ideal order among themselves, which is modified by the introduction of the new (the really new) work of art among them" (*Selected Essays* [London: Faber, 1951] p. 15). The Borges essay was first brought to my attention by Bert O. States, for whom Augustine is a created precursor of Beckett. See *The Shape of Paradox: An Essay on Waiting for Godot* (Berkeley: Univ. of California Press, 1978), pp. 94–95, n. 4.

3. *The Family Letters of Samuel Butler, 1841–1886*, ed. Arnold Silver (Stanford: Stanford Univ. Press, 1962), pp. 89–90.

4. "A Victorian Son," in *The Living Novel and Later Appreciations* (New York: Random, 1964), pp. 140–41.

CHAPTER I

1. *An Inquiry Concerning the Principles of Morals*, ed. Charles W. Hendel (Indianapolis: Bobbs-Merrill, 1957), p. 10.

2. *The Natural History of Religion*, ed. H. E. Root (London, 1956; rpt. Stanford Univ. Press, 1957), p. 41; *Dialogues Concerning Natural Religion*, ed. Norman Kemp Smith (Oxford, 1935; rpt. Indianapolis: Bobbs-Merrill, 1977), p. 154. Cleanthes speaks these last words, but when they are compared to some of Philo's remarks later on (see, e.g., p. 174), as well as to the opening of *The Natural History*, it is evident that for once Cleanthes is speaking for Hume himself.

3. *Dialogues*, pp. 227, 202.

4. *Natural History*, p. 42.

5. All etymologies are taken from *The American Heritage Dictionary*, ed. William Morris (Boston: Houghton Mifflin, 1978).

6. "Preface," *Back to Methuselah* (1921; rpt. Baltimore: Penguin, 1961), pp. 62–63.

7. Consider Miss Savage's irreverent anecdote: "A clergyman was examining the children of a village school in the parable of the good Samaritan, and after explaining that priest meant clergyman, asked why did the priest go by on the other side. 'Please Sir', said one boy, 'because he had been robbed already'." The "he" of course is the man who had fallen among thieves, though it took Butler and Jones a while to see it. Once they did, Butler asked Miss Savage, "Would you mind telling the story to my father." See *Letters Between Samuel Butler and Miss E.M.A. Savage, 1871–1885*, ed. Geoffrey Keynes and Brian Hill (London: Cape, 1935), pp. 308–9.

8. See *The Notebooks*, Vol. XX of *The Shrewsbury Edition of the Works of Samuel Butler*, ed. Henry Festing Jones and A.T. Bartholomew (London: Cape, 1926), p. 189. Hereafter referred to parenthetically as *N*.

The refusal of Theobald or of Cambridge dons to look at the evidence making against the assumptions underlying the Thirty-nine Articles — even when a part of their brain tells them the evidence is heavy — was of course typical of Victorian Christians, of whatever confession. The well-meaning among them led lives of what Walter E. Houghton has called "sincere insincerity," or what their contemporary critics and their Stracheyan biographers have more sweepingly called "hypocrisy." (See Houghton's *The Victorian Frame of Mind, 1830–1870* [New Haven: Yale Univ. Press, 1957], pp. 394–430.) Theobald is not like Tartuffe, who shams piety to gain material advantages; he is like Bulstrode in *Middlemarch*, who really believes that his material advantages are a consequence of his deeply felt piety. The motivation toward not looking at the evidence for or against religion will be overwhelming when, as Hazlitt points out, the believer risks so much even by looking at himself: "A religious man is afraid of looking into the state of his soul, lest at the same time he should reveal it to Heaven; and tries to persuade himself that by shutting his eyes to his true character and feelings, they will remain a profound secret both here and hereafter. This is a strong engine and irresistible inducement to self-deception ..." ("On Cant and Hypocrisy," [1828], rpt. in *Selected Essays of William Hazlitt, 1778–1830*, ed. Geoffrey Keynes [London: Nonesuch, 1934], p. 365). This is to apply to introspection what, in *Little Dorrit*, Mrs. General applies to sexuality, poverty, venality, etc. — a primly tied blindfold.

9. *Ernest Pontifex; or The Way of All Flesh*, ed. Daniel F. Howard (Boston: Houghton Mifflin, 1964), p. 227. Hereafter referred to parenthetically as *WAF*. Except for purposes of catching certain ironies, I shall avoid the circumlocutions involved in distinguishing Butler from his personae Overton and Ernest in *WAF*, or from the personae in *The Fair Haven* or *Erewhon*.

Mr. Howard's notes indicate passages Butler deleted, usually to cut redundancies, but sometimes to add to or subtract from the bitterness he felt toward his several enemies. The whole of Mr. Howard's work in this edition is exemplary.

10. *An Inquiry Concerning Human Understanding*, ed. Charles W. Hendel (Indianapolis: Bobbs-Merrill, 1955), p. 123.

11. "The Evolution of Childhood," in *The History of Childhood*, ed. Lloyd deMause (1974; rpt. New York: Harper, 1975), p. 10.

12. "The New World of Children in Eighteenth-Century England," *Past and Present*, 67 (May 1975), 92.

13. *The Medea*, 1029–35. DeMause refers to this passage, but again he oversimplifies the parental villainy. Medea is extremely unamiable, of course, but Euripides does

have her speak of less "self-willed" (1028) reasons to withhold her hand, including the distant prospect of seeing her children happy in their marriages, and the near one of embracing them in her arms: "How delicate the skin, how sweet the breath of children!" (1075, trans. Rex Warner).

14. See deMause, pp. 25–32.

15. The undifferentiation of father and son in mimetic rivalry is a major theme in René Girard's *Violence and the Sacred*, trans. Patrick Gregory (Baltimore: Johns Hopkins Univ. Press, 1977).

16. *Samuel Butler's Notebooks*, ed. Geoffrey Keynes and Brian Hill (London: Cape, 1951), pp. 189, 74. This edition joins entries from the Shrewsbury *Notebooks*, A. T. Bartholomew's 1934 volume of *Further Extracts*, Jones's *Memoir*, the Nonesuch *Butleriana* (1932), and the unpublished manuscript notebooks. It is in all the best source for some otherwise hard to locate material. A definitive edition of *The Notebooks* has been prepared by Hans-Peter Breuer and R. E. Parsell, and is forthcoming from the Open University Press in England.

17. "The Butlerian Inheritance of Shaw," *The Dalhousie Review*, 41 (1961), 170. The comfortable childhood Mr. Bissell describes was indeed the heritage of many Victorians who in their adult years had to redefine God, or to lose him altogether. One thinks of the childhoods depicted in Froude's *Nemesis of Faith*, or in *David Copperfield*, *Pendennis*, *The Mill on the Floss*, or in Blake's *Songs of Innocence*: not that these early years are untroubled, but that they are a time when the child can talk confidingly with the heavenly Father, go to Sunday service happily with the earthly one, and feel cared for by both.

18. *The Fair Haven*, Vol. III of *The Shrewsbury Edition* (1923), pp. 8–9. Hereafter referred to parenthetically as *FH*.

19. *Notebooks*, ed. Keynes and Hill, p. 119.

20. Ibid., pp. 87, 34.

21. That Butler's "true" Christ is not altogether his own invention is at least plausible upon a fresh, un-Paulinized reading of the Gospels — the sort of reading Shaw undertakes in his eloquent "Preface" (1915) to *Androcles and the Lion*, the section entitled "The Savage John and the Civilized Jesus": "He told straitlaced disciples that they would have trouble enough from other people without making any for themselves, and that they should avoid martyrdom and enjoy themselves whilst they had the chance. 'When they persecute you in this city,' he says, 'flee to the next.' ... He is convivial, feasting with Roman officials and sinners. He is careless of his person, and is remonstrated with for not washing his hands before sitting down to table.... Like the late Samuel Butler, he regards disease as a department of sin, and on curing a lame man, says 'Thy sins are forgiven' instead of 'Arise and walk,' subsequently maintaining, when the Scribes reproach him for assuming power to forgive sin as well as to cure disease, that the two come to the same thing. He has no modest affectations, and claims to be greater than Solomon or Jonah. When reproached, as Bunyan was, for resorting to the art of fiction when teaching in parables, he justifies himself on the ground that art is the only way in which the people can be taught. He is, in short, what we should call an artist and a Bohemian in his manner of life." See *Selected Plays with Prefaces* (New York: Dodd, Mead, 1948), pp. 768–69.

22. *Erewhon Revisited*, Vol. XVI of *The Shrewsbury Edition* (1925), pp. 220–21.

23. See "Thought and Language," in *Collected Essays, Volume Two*, Vol. XIX of *The Shrewsbury Edition* (1925), pp. 69–80. Though some critics have complained of what they regard as the pettiness of Butler's verbal inversions (see Peter Coveney, *The Image*

of Childhood, introd. F. R. Leavis [1957; rpt. Baltimore: Penguin, 1967], p. 289; David Grylls, *Guardians and Angels: Parents and Children in Nineteenth-Century Literature* [London: Faber, 1978], p. 167), I think Clara Stillman is correct in distinguishing his practice from the trifling of, say, W. S. Gilbert. She writes: "Words have a history, an evolution, a store of conscious and unconscious associations, a soul of meanings that have died and been reborn in slightly altered forms, secret kinships with other words apparently alien and with thoughts in process of birth or not yet born.... [So] when he spoke of living under grace, or of the life of the world to come, he not only endowed these phrases with a richly modern biological and psychological content, but he subtly suggested that these were the eternal meanings which had always resided in them consciously unrecognized but unconsciously accepted" (pp. 211–12).

24. *Life and Habit,* Vol. IV of *The Shrewsbury Edition* (1923), pp. 32–33. Hereafter referred to parenthetically as *LH.*

25. *The Natural History,* pp. 52–53.

26. *Culture and Anarchy,* ed. J. Dover Wilson (Cambridge, Eng.: Cambridge Univ. Press, 1932), pp. 57–58.

CHAPTER II

1. *Butler and Darwin: Two Versions of Evolution* (New York: Harcourt, 1960), p. 38.

2. Simpson writes: "One may say, if one wishes, that sodium 'knows' how to combine with chlorine to make salt, that an embryo 'knows' how to develop into an adult and that a pianist 'knows' how to play a composition. But the nature and source of the 'knowledge' are so completely different in the three cases that use of the same word, 'knows,' becomes only a metaphor or a pun... Butler mistook his word game for truth." See "Lamarck, Darwin and Butler: Three Approaches to Evolution," *The American Scholar,* 30 (1961), 248. To be fair, Simpson also challenges the metaphors of "coding" and "information" used in DNA research, but one is puzzled what kind of language, short of one consisting purely of mathematical symbols, he *would* find appropriate to scientific discourse. The biologist's felt need for an anthropomorphic language suggests that Butler may have been right in insisting that sodium "knows" how to combine with chlorine in a way that is *analogous to* a man's knowing how to play the piano.

3. With Kingsley's leave, but without naming him, Darwin included the following sentence from a letter in the preface to the second edition of *The Origin:* "I have gradually learnt to see that it is just as noble a conception of Deity to believe that He created animal forms capable of self-development into all forms needful...as to believe that He required a fresh act of intervention to supply the lacunae which He Himself had made. I question whether the former be not the loftier thought." See Brenda Colloms, *Charles Kingsley: The Lion of Eversley* (London: Constable, 1975), pp. 243–44. Butler took the phrase "self-development" with more seriousness than Darwin, in this harmless sop to the religious reader, ever did.

4. "Preface" to *Back to Methuselah,* p. 39. Darwin himself noted that "natural selection" is a misleading phrase, for it suggests the very opposite of what he was trying to demonstrate: that Nature doesn't exist, and that she wouldn't select if she did. See A. Dwight Culler, "The Darwinian Revolution and Literary Form," in *The Art of Victorian Prose,* ed. George Levine and William Madden (New York: Oxford Univ. Press, 1968), p. 245. Though I find myself taking issue with Mr. Culler below (n. 5), I wouldn't want to obscure the debt every student of Victorian prose owes to this shrewd essay, as indeed to everything Mr. Culler has written.

Recent evolutionists have been reluctant to admit that there is a real issue between Darwin and the vitalists. Ernst Mayr, for instance, writes: "Many opponents of Darwinism failed to understand the complementary roles of variation and selection and protested that Darwin had postulated a brute, mechanical, soulless universe, depending on the whims of accident....[But] survival, the ability to contribute to the genetic content of the next generation, is not at all a matter of accident, but *a statistically predictable property* of the genotype. The immense power and universal occurrence of natural selection have, in the meantime, been demonstrated by thousands of modern selection experiments and by controlled observations of individually marked natural populations. That natural selection is a direction-giving force, within the limitations of the evolutionary potential set for a given species by its genotype, has now been substantiated abundantly. It is now apparent how absurd is the glib claim that Darwinism expounds the production of perfection by accident, the rule of 'higgledy-piggledy,' as Samuel Butler called it" ("Introduction" to Charles Darwin, *On the Origin of Species: A Facsimile of the First Edition* [Cambridge, Mass.: Harvard Univ. Press, 1964], pp. xvi–xvii [italics added]). I would submit that "thousands" of experiments demonstrating the statistical predictability of variations do not reveal a purposive intelligence at work among those variations — which is what Butler and the other vitalists were holding out for. One might as well say that the knitting done by Hardy's Immanent Will discloses a providential plan, just by virtue of the repetitive patterned stitch it has "wrought by rapt aesthetic rote," by "automatic sense / Unweeting why or whence." Hardy knew there is neither thought nor solace in properties that can be surveyed for their statistical predictability:
  Rather they ["things terrene"] show that,
    like a knitter drowsed,
  Whose fingers play in skilled unmindfulness,
  The Will has woven with an absent heed
  Since life first was; and ever will so weave. (*The Dynasts*, Pt. I, "Fore Scene")
That, Butler would insist, is Darwinism imaged forth with appropriate dismay.

  5. Mr. Culler argues that "The Book of Machines," "although using Darwinian materials, is really a satire on modern technology and also on the process of reasoning by analogy as exemplified in Joseph Butler's *Analogy* ..." (p. 233). The question of Butler's intentions in *Erewhon* with respect to Darwin is extremely vexed. Mr. Culler must have in mind Butler's letter to Darwin, where he says: "When I first got hold of the idea [of 'The Chapter upon Machines'], I developed it for mere fun and because it amused me and I thought would amuse others, but without a particle of serious meaning; but I developed it and introduced it into *Erewhon* with the intention of implying: 'See how easy it is to be plausible, and what absurd propositions can be defended by a little ingenuity and distortion and departure from strictly scientific methods,' and I had Butler's *Analogy* in my head as the book at which it should be aimed, but preferred to conceal my aim for many reasons." See Henry Festing Jones, *Samuel Butler...A Memoir* (London: Macmillan, 1919), I, 156. But playing with an idea "for mere fun" led him into insights which suddenly required a serious look — just as in *Life and Habit* he picked up a "pebble" Lamarck had dropped, "turned it over and over for...amusement," and discovered, as it grew brighter, that "the trifle which I had picked up idly had proved to be a talisman of inestimable value..." (*LH*, 250). The pebble which he played with in *Erewhon* appeared, on backward glance, to be the very talismanic *reductio ad absurdum* of Darwinism which, in his preface to the second edition (1872), he had denied it to be. This is evident when, summarizing the *oeuvre* in

1902, he writes: "With *Erewhon* Charles Darwin smelt danger from afar.... He knew very well that the machine chapters in *Erewhon* would not end there..." (Jones, II, 382). I read *Erewhon* "backwards" from, say, the end of *Life and Habit*, for in it are the seeds of revolt against Darwin, the full implications of which Butler only gradually awakened to. This certainly is the way the book strikes P. N. Furbank, who aptly says: "In *Darwin Among the Machines* [the early form of 'The Book of the Machines'] he had found the proper way to make things awkward for the Darwinians. Attack the theory from the outside and it can defend itself without much discomfort; but go inside the theory, follow up its suggestions to their logical conclusion, make amendments to the theory as so to give it a dubious sort of compatibility with religion, and the defenders of the theory are irretrievably committed to what they most wished to avoid, a discussion upon theological ground." See *Samuel Butler* (Cambridge, Eng.: Cambridge Univ. Press, 1948), p. 61.

6. As U. C. Knoepflmacher points out, the card game is "a superb parody of the fortuitous process of Darwinian selection" (*Religious Humanism and the Victorian Novel: George Eliot, Walter Pater, and Samuel Butler* [Princeton: Princeton University Press, 1965], p. 272). It is true that Christina, like most women in the nineteenth century, has a very narrow range of choices as to how she shall live her life. Butler feels that she errs, however, in supposing herself to have *no* choices, and in thus letting the cards tell her what to do.

7. *Dialogues*, p. 174.

8. *The Natural History*, p. 21.

9. "Samuel Butler: *The Way of All Flesh*," in *An Introduction to the English Novel*, II (London: Hutchinson, 1953), 44.

10. *Samuel Butler: A Mid-Victorian Modern*, p. 144. Butler would agree with Schiller and his Victorian disciple, Carlyle: life's purpose, its truth, "*immer wird, nie ist.*" See Carlyle's "Characteristics," *Critical and Miscellaneous Essays*, ed. H. D. Traill (New York: Scribner's, 1896–1901), III, 38. I am indebted to Houghton (p. 30) for drawing my attention to this passage.

11. *Dialogues*, pp. 211–12, 210.

12. *Notebooks*, ed. Keynes and Hill, p. 255.

13. *Dialogues*, p. 167.

14. "God the Known and God the Unknown," *Collected Essays, Volume One*, Vol. XVIII of *The Shrewsbury Edition* (1925), pp. 37–38.

15. Butler imagines how the remnant of men who will survive the next ice age might live: "...a simple people, busy hunting shellfish on the drying ocean beds, and with little time for introspection; yet they can read and write and sum, for by that time these accomplishments will have become universal, and will be acquired as easily as we now learn to talk; but they do so as a matter of course, and without self-consciousness. Also they make the simpler kinds of machinery too easily to be able to follow their own operations — the manner of their own apprenticeship being to them as a buried city. May we not imagine that, after the lapse of another ten thousand years or so, some one of them may again become cursed with lust of introspection, and a second Harvey may astonish the world by discovering that it can read and write, and that steam-engines do not grow, but are made? It may be safely prophesied that he will die a martyr, and be honoured in the fourth generation" (*LH*, 47–48).

16. *Butler and Darwin*, p. 109.

17. *Erewhon*, ed. Peter Mudford (Baltimore: Penguin, 1970), pp. 147, 154–55. Hereafter referred to parenthetically as *E*. This is the best cheap edition, based on that

of 1901, which has some sixty pages of additional material Butler introduced in order to renew his copyright. This padding makes for much repetition, and for no startlingly new ideas, but one can note Butler's increased amusement at one response to Darwin's view of nature, namely, the excesses of vegetarians. See chapters 26–27, which Shaw could perhaps have read with more profit. A definitive edition of *Erewhon* has been edited by Hans-Peter Breuer and Daniel F. Howard, and is forthcoming from the University of Delaware Press. Part of Mr. Howard's excellent introduction has been published in the *Samuel Butler Newsletter*, 2 (Spring 1978), 1–12.

18. Although Alethaea is real enough to Overton, as his account of her burial shows (*WAF*, 135), Ernest himself has very little reaction to her death. She is more substantial than some critics have supposed (see below, pp. 60–62), but she is there for one principal reason: to leave her money to her godson and nephew. Butler may well *mean* her to be mostly a convenience, inasmuch as he wishes to assert that money is more important to the Pontifex family than is the personality of any one member. Alethaea "sacrifices" herself for the sake of her strain within the species.

19. Butler's self-contempt is evident in his notes on Towneley's original: "Pauli's clothes must have cost twice as much as mine did. Everything he had was good, and he was such a fine, handsome fellow, with such an attractive manner, that to me he seemed everything that I should like myself to be, but knew very well that I was not. I knew myself to be plebian in appearance and believed myself to be more plebian in tastes than I probably was...Perhaps the secret of it all lay in the fact of my knowing well that I had not passed by the ambush of young days scatheless, whereas I could see (and I imagine truly) that to Pauli there had been no ambush of young days at all. The main desire of my life was to conceal how severely I had been wounded, and to get beyond the reach of those arrows that from time to time still reached me." See "Charles Paine Pauli and Samuel Butler," ed. Desmond MacCarthy, *Life and Letters*, 7 (1931), 254–56.

20. *The Natural History*, p. 32.

CHAPTER III

1. "Of Atheism," in *Selected Writings of Francis Bacon*, ed. Hugh G. Dick (New York: Modern Library-Random, 1955), p. 44.

2. "Samuel Butler: The New Life Reviewed," in *The Works of Bernard Shaw* (London: Constable, 1931), XXIX, 61.

3. See Chap. II, n. 5. One is not only well-advised to read *Erewhon* as the initiation of Butler's revolt against Darwin; one is well-advised not to assume that every Erewhonian institution is being endorsed when it is opposite to its English counterpart, and condemned when it is similar. Butler's satire requires a more agile response.

What Butler calls the Darwinian equation between fortune and virtue, misfortune and vice, was in fact a Victorian commonplace. See Bulwer Lytton's remark: "In other countries poverty is a misfortune, — with us it is a crime" (*England and the English* [1833; rpt. London, 1874], p. 33, quoted by Houghton, p. 185, n. 9. Houghton also instances passages in a similar vein from Thomas Hughes, John Sterling, and Emerson). Lytton was widely presumed to have written *Erewhon* when it first appeared anonymously.

4. Because he doesn't mark the seed of Butler's enmity toward Darwin, Mr. Culler I think misses this distinction between the Erewhonian treatments of physical and mental disorders. He writes: "Negatively, we are told that it is no more foolish to be angry with a man for having a bad cold, which he can't help, than it is to be angry with

him for having bad intentions, which presumably he can't help either; and positively, we are told that it is quite as sensible to try to cure a man of embezzling as it is to cure him of tuberculosis" (p. 235).

5. Mencken writes: "There is, as a matter of fact, not the least reason to believe that cutting down the death-rate, in itself, is of much benefit to the human race. A people with an annual rate of 40 a thousand might still produce many Huxleys and Darwins, and one with a rate of but 8 or 9 might produce nothing but Coolidges and Billy Sundays.... [W]hat is too often forgotten is that nature obviously intends the botched to die, and that every interference with that benign process is full of dangers." See *Prejudices: A Selection*, ed. James T. Farrell (New York: Vintage-Random, 1958), pp. 249–50.

6. Grylls, pp. 161–63.

7. Butler disliked professional transcendentalists: "The Athenians poisoned Socrates; and Aristophanes — than whom few more profoundly religious men have ever been born — did not, so far as we can gather, think the worse of his countrymen on that account. It is not improbable that if they had poisoned Plato too, Aristophanes would have been well enough pleased; but I think he would have preferred either of these two men to Marcus Aurelius" (*LH*, 238–39).

8. *Nicomachean Ethics* (1153b), trans. Martin Ostwald (Indianapolis: Bobbs-Merrill, 1962), pp. 208–9.

9. "Letter to Menoeceus" (131b), in *Letters, Principal Doctrines, and Vatican Sayings*, trans. Russell M. Geer (Indianapolis: Bobbs-Merrill, 1964), pp. 57–58. Butler's extension of Epicureanism, somewhat in despite of the extant writings, may be truer to Epicurus than those writings would allow. Cf. Remy de Gourmont, who in *Une Nuit au Luxembourg* writes: "My friend, for some centuries now the schools have been poisoning your sensibilities and strangling your intelligence by making you believe that the pleasures of Epicurus were exclusively pleasures of the mind. Epicurus was too wise to disdain any sort of pleasure. He wanted to know, and he did know, all the satisfactions which can become the satisfactions of men; he abused nothing, but he used everything, in his life of harmony." Quoted in Kenneth Burke, *Counter-Statement*, 3rd ed. (Berkeley: Univ. of California Press, 1968), p. 22.

10. Quoted by Richard B. Brandt, "Hedonism," in *The Encyclopedia of Philosophy*, ed. Paul Edwards (New York: Macmillan, 1967), III, 433.

11. *Nicomachean Ethics* (1153b), p. 209.

12. G. N. Sharma, in "Samuel Butler and Edmund Burke: A Comparative Study in British Conservatism," *The Dalhousie Review*, 53, No. 1 (1973), 5–29, has argued for another, also unconscious, affinity.

13. *A Treatise of Human Nature*, ed. L. A. Selby-Bigge (Oxford: Clarendon, 1888), pp. 468–69.

14. Ibid., p. 486; *Inquiry Concerning Morals*, p. 45.

15. *Treatise*, pp. 489, 492, 486–87, 500.

16. *Inquiry Concerning Morals*, pp. 89, 158, 90, 6. Cf. Carl L. Becker, *The Heavenly City of the Eighteenth-Century Philosophers* (New Haven: Yale Univ. Press, 1932), p. 87, on the philosophers' need, under the threat of atheism, to reassert some definition of innate human nature, whether Hume's "sympathy" or Rousseau's "heart."

17. *Inquiry Concerning Morals*, p. 8.

18. Cf. Robert Shafer, *Christianity and Naturalism* (New Haven: Yale Univ. Press, 1926), p. 230.

19. *Treatise*, pp. 596–97, 600, 598. Cf. Clara Middleton in Meredith's *The Egoist*, who

"preferred to be herself, with the egoism of women!" (ch. 6) — a salutary egoism obviously to be urged against the sexual imperialism of Willoughby Patterne. Meredith and Butler are hardly alone among nineteenth-century English novelists in recognizing the need for a proper egoism. To take but two instances: Emma Woodhouse has too large and Dorothea Brooke too small a degree of self-love at the beginnings of their stories, and a large part of what follows in them is meant to teach each her due degree.

20. *Inquiry Concerning Morals*, p. 96.

21. "What a beast a man must be too who leaves his money in this way [to found a college or a scholarship]. I wonder he is not ashamed to tell the world that he has died without having seen one person whom he has loved well enough to let him have his money when he can no longer use it himself. Look at Erasmus Wilson who has just died and left his money to the College of Surgeons — what an awful thing to do" (*Notebooks*, ed. Keynes and Hill, pp. 18–19).

22. *Letters Between*, p. 255.

23. Jones, II, 211.

24. "Samuel Butler," *The Edinburgh Review*, 231 (1920), 62.

25. "The Butlerian Inheritance of Shaw," p. 167.

26. U. C. Knoepflmacher, in *Laughter and Despair: Readings in Ten Novels of the Victorian Era* (Berkeley: Univ. of California Press, 1971), p. 211, has also noted the etymological significance of Ernest's surname. Its priestly suggestions are evident too. Cf. Carlyle's usage, which conflates the two meanings: "Never perhaps since our first Bridge-builders, Sin and Death, built that stupendous Arch from Hell-gate to the Earth, did any Pontifex, or Pontiff, undertake such a task as the present Editor" (*Sartor Resartus* [London: Everyman-Dent, 1908], Pt. I, Ch. xi [p. 59]).

27. *Treatise*, p. 526.

28. "Preface," *Back to Methuselah*, p. 55.

29. Coveney, p. 288.

30. *Principia Ethica* (Cambridge, Eng.: Cambridge Univ. Press, 1903), pp. 73–81.

31. *Nicomachean Ethics* (1153b), p. 208.

32. Cf. William K. Frankena, *Ethics* (Englewood Cliffs, N.J.: Prentice-Hall, 1963), p. 70.

CHAPTER IV

1. See Coveney, deMause, Grylls, Plumb, passim.

2. Quoted in *An Anthology of original documents written between 1700 and 1815*, comp. Asa Briggs, Vol. III of *How They Lived* (New York: Barnes & Noble, 1969), p. 270. Mr. Briggs cites *The Tatler*, 1706, but since that magazine's numbers didn't begin till 1709, this must be an error. The very thorough index of G. A. Aitken's four volume edition (Oxford: Clarendon, 1898–99) hasn't enabled me to find the original passage. The reference was first brought to my attention by deMause (p. 16), who doesn't notice the error in dating.

3. *The Reasonableness of Christianity*, ed. I. T. Ramsey (Stanford: Stanford Univ. Press, 1958), par. 242 (p. 64). With respect to infanticide, even Aristotle sounds like a strict social Darwinist: "As to exposing or rearing the children born, let there be a law that no deformed child shall be reared; but on the ground of number of children, if the regular customs hinder any of those born being exposed, there must be a limit filed to the procreation of offspring." Quoted by deMause, p. 26.

4. DeMause, p. 17.

5. *The Authority of the Bible* (New York: Harper, 1929), p. 228.

6. *The Reasonableness*, pars. 2–6 (pp. 26–28).

7. *The Educational Writings of John Locke*, ed. James L. Axtell (Cambridge, Eng.: Cambridge Univ. Press, 1968), pp. 159, 114–15.

8. *The Letters of Philip Dormer Stanhope, 4th Earl of Chesterfield*, ed. Bonamy Dobrée (London: Eyre & Spottiswoode, 1932), III, 784.

9. Ibid., III, 777, 1115; II, 504.

10. *The Educational Writings*, p. 191.

11. *The Letters of Chesterfield*, III, 1030.

12. *The Educational Writings*, pp. 191, 195–96.

13. *The Letters of Chesterfield*, IV, 1229.

14. Jones, I, 46.

15. *The Letters of Chesterfield*, III, 699.

16. Basil Willey, in his *The Eighteenth Century Background* (London, 1940; rpt. Boston: Beacon, 1961), p. 123, has briefly linked Butler, Chesterfield, and Hume on this theme of High Ydgrunitism: "Your virtue may be described as 'my approval of you'; my virtue is 'your approval of me.'" On the dilemmas faced by the liberal churchman, see Butler's "A Clergyman's Doubts," in *N*, 308–13.

17. See G. N. Sharma, "Samuel Butler and Edmund Burke," passim.

18. *Alps and Sanctuaries*, Vol. VII of *The Shrewsbury Edition* (1924), p. 51.

19. *Cobbett's Advice to Young Men and (Incidentally) to Young Women* (New York: Doyle, 1831), pp. 194–95, 213, 236–37, 221, 214, 227–28.

CHAPTER V

1. Mr. Buckley writes that "the two objectives do not always coincide, for the first involves the relation of the individual to his inheritance and the second defends the hero's right to assert his complete independence of his father and mother and of all the traditions and pieties, natural or not, they represent." See *Season of Youth* (Cambridge, Mass.: Harvard Univ. Press, 1974), p. 123.

Butler argues that though Ernest is a man, there is no *one* way for him to mature; that though he is a Pontifex, there is no *one* way for him to carry the family's heritage. Butler's instinctive dislike for *Wilhelm Meister* may have something to do with Goethe's contrary view, that there is a *normative* way to be human, European, German, and so on. (See *Letters Between*, p. 98.) Against Goethe's (or Arnold's) notion that an ideal man can be built up out of harmoniously interrelated parts, Butler, like Mill, favors the development of the *individual* man, whose *Bildung* is at many points peculiar to him, not modeled after some Idea. See Houghton, pp. 287–91, for an incisive discussion of Hellenic vs. Romantic concepts of self-development.

2. *Psychoanalysis and the Unconscious*, introd. Philip Rieff (New York: Viking, 1960), pp. 9, 15, 31.

3. The need for an intelligently conscious ego has gone unnoticed in the Butler criticism, and understandably so, given his express emphasis on the powers of unconscious memory which Mr. Knoepflmacher has sharply focused on: "...while Arnold, Pater, and George Eliot appeal to conscience as a guide for morality, Butler stresses the power of the unconscious....By paring down Arnold's 'power not ourselves' into a 'power within ourselves,' the instinctive wisdom or 'cunning' he venerated as a life-force, he provided a transition to the vitalism of George Bernard Shaw or D. H. Lawrence." See *Religious Humanism and the Victorian Novel: George Eliot, Walter Pater, and Samuel Butler* (Princeton: Princeton Univ. Press, 1965), p. 255.

4. Kettle writes that in Ernest's cutting of his parents Butler has indicated our need for revolutionary action: "It is his realisation — a realisation which, on the basis of his past experience, we share — that in order to live decently, to achieve self-respect and avoid further degradation, he must cut away totally from the ties and values of the bourgeois world and his determination, on the strength of this 'warning voice', to learn a trade and change his class-allegiance; this is the most striking revelation of The Way of All Flesh." See An Introduction to the English Novel, II, 43. As I discuss below, this is the sort of inference Shaw draws from the novel — an inference which Butler might have been reluctant to endorse, but which is not alien to the ideas his novel has sounded.

5. The Educational Writings, p. 202.

6. Wilson, "The Satire of Samuel Butler," The Shores of Light (New York: Farrar, Straus, and Giroux, 1952), p. 563; Kettle, p. 42; Letters Between, p. 96.

7. Inquiry Concerning Morals, pp. 72–73.

8. James Boswell, Life of Johnson, ed. R. W. Chapman, 3rd ed. (London: Oxford Univ. Press, 1970), pp. 311, 1185.

9. "Thought and Language," p. 80.

10. "The Legacy of Samuel Butler," The Listener (12 June 1952), 956.

11. "Preface" to Major Barbara, in Selected Plays with Prefaces, pp. 309–10.

12. Mr. Furbank remarks: "Money is typical of the stolen birthright. It is something taken by force in the course of the imaginary patricide. And being taken by force, it comes to represent force in itself. It becomes a talisman as well as a trophy....The notion of the breaking into the guarded orchard, and the carrying off of the prize, apply commonly to sexual matters, while here they are felt more strongly in regard to money" (pp. 20–21). I would add that not only sexual but also philosophical quarrels devolve into the financial quarrel because money and the things it can buy give the emotionally exhausted and bewildered Butler something palpable — "a talisman as well as a trophy" — to seize. At his weakest, he looks in danger of reverting to the materialism for which he has castigated Darwin.

13. Mr. Buckley too readily assumes Ernest's (and, by extension, Butler's) ignorance of his emotional disability: "Though only Aunt Alethea has given the child Ernest a truly disinterested affection, it is still disconcerting to see the unloved boy become the loveless man with no sense of his deficiency" (pp. 132–33). The good Butlerian reader should, however, be alert to the possibilities of unconscious knowledge — how it works, and what it can do for the ego. We have to say that Butler (and Ernest, who is supposed to be reviewing his history in conversations with Overton) both does and doesn't have a "sense of his deficiency."

CHAPTER VI

1. Towneley is a sphex wasp in human form: "Why should the generations overlap one another at all? Why cannot we be buried as eggs in neat little cells with ten or twenty thousands pounds each wrapped round us in Bank of England notes, and wake up, as the sphex wasp does, to find that its papa and mamma have not only left ample provision at its elbow but have been eaten by sparrows some weeks before we began to live consciously on our own accounts?" (WAF, 71).

2. Alps and Sanctuaries, p. 131.

3. "Samuel Butler: The New Life Reviewed," pp. 56–57, 66. Similarly pitying denunciations can be found in Gosse, p. 57, and J. Middleton Murry, Aspects of Literature (London: Collins, 1920), p. 120.

4. *Alps and Sanctuaries*, p. 135.

5. "How to Make the Best of Life," *Collected Essays, Volume Two*, pp. 98–99.

6. "Samuel Butler: The New Life Reviewed," p. 64.

7. *Jacob's Room* (1922; rpt. New York: Harcourt, 1959), pp. 108–9.

8. *Contemporary Writers* (New York: Harcourt, 1965), p. 29. Woolf continues that "if today we are less ambitious, less apt to be solemn and sentimental, and display without shame a keener appetite for happiness, we owe this very largely to Butler's example" (p. 31). And in another review essay: "Then, again, we had fancied that some idea or other was our own breeding. But here, on the next page, was Butler's original version, from which our seed had blown. If you want to come up afresh in thousands of minds and books long after you are dead, no doubt the way to do it is to start thinking for yourself. The novels that have been fertilized by *The Way of All Flesh* must by this time constitute a large library, with well-known names upon their backs" (p. 35).

Woolf prizes Butler as a splendid amateur flourishing in an era of increasing specialization. G. M. Young reminds us, though, that what we would call Butler's interdisciplinary achievement was not uncommon in the Victorian Age, and that the specialization that was evident after say 1870 was negligible compared to what was to come a generation later: "[W]here [he laments] shall we look for the successors of the Mills and Ruskins and Tennysons? Or of the public for which they wrote? The common residual intelligence is becoming impoverished for the benefit of the specialist, the technician, and the aesthete: we leave behind us the world of historical ironmasters and banker historians, with its genial watchword: to know something of everything and everything of something: and through the gateway of the Competitive Examination we go out into the Waste Land of Experts, each knowing so much about so little that he can neither be contradicted nor is worth contradicting." (See *Victorian England: Portrait of an Age*, Second Edition [London: Oxford Univ. Press, 1953], p. 160.)

9. *Private Papers of James Boswell*, ed. Geoffrey Scott and Frederick A. Pottle, Vol. XII (1931), pp. 227–32. Quoted in introduction to *Dialogues Concerning Natural Religion*, pp. 76–79.

10. "Introduction" to Coveney, p. 27.

11. A good collation of references may be found in the otherwise merely gossipy William Van O'Connor, "Samuel Butler and Bloomsbury," *From Jane Austen to Joseph Conrad*, ed. Robert C. Rathburn and Martin Steinmann, Jr. (Minneapolis: Univ. of Minnesota Press, 1958), pp. 257–73. For Butler's influence on Forster see Lee Elbert Holt, "E. M. Forster and Samuel Butler," *PMLA*, 61 (1946), 804–19, with discussion of *Howards End* on pp. 813–16.

12. *The English Moralists* (New York: Norton, 1964), p. 282.

13. *The Letters of D. H. Lawrence*, ed. Aldous Huxley (New York: Viking, 1932), p. 66.

Selected Bibliography

Aristotle. *Nicomachean Ethics.* Trans. Martin Ostwald. Indianapolis: Bobbs-Merrill, 1962.

Arnold, Matthew. *Culture and Anarchy.* Ed. J. Dover Wilson. Cambridge, Eng.: Cambridge Univ. Press, 1932.

Becker, Carl. *The Heavenly City of the Eighteenth-Century Philosophers.* New Haven: Yale Univ. Press, 1932.

Bissell, Claude T. "The Butlerian Inheritance of Shaw." *The Dalhousie Review,* 41 (1961), 159–73.

———. "A Study of *The Way of All Flesh.*" In *Nineteenth-Century Studies.* Ed. Herbert Davis, et al. Ithaca: Cornell Univ. Press, 1940.

Boswell, James. *Life of Johnson.* Ed. R. W. Chapman. 3rd ed. London: Oxford Univ. Press, 1970.

Buckley, Jerome Hamilton. *Season of Youth: The Bildungsroman from Dickens to Golding.* Cambridge, Mass.: Harvard Univ. Press, 1974.

Butler, Samuel. *Alps and Sanctuaries.* Vol. VII of *The Shrewsbury Edition of the Works of Samuel Butler.* Ed. Henry Festing Jones and A. T. Bartholomew. London: Cape, 1924.

———. *Collected Essays.* Vols. XVIII and XIX of *The Shrewsbury Edition.* 1925.

———. *Erewhon.* Ed. Peter Mudford. Baltimore: Penguin, 1970.

———. *Erewhon Revisited.* Vol. XVI of *The Shrewsbury Edition.* 1925.

———. *Ernest Pontifex; or The Way of All Flesh.* Ed. Daniel F. Howard. Boston: Houghton Mifflin, 1964.

———. *The Fair Haven.* Vol. III of *The Shrewsbury Edition.* 1923.

———. *Life and Habit.* Vol. IV of *The Shrewsbury Edition.* 1923.

———. *The Notebooks.* Vol. XX of *The Shrewsbury Edition.* 1926.

———. *Samuel Butler's Notebooks.* Ed. Geoffrey Keynes and Brian Hill. London: Cape, 1951.

Chesterfield, Philip Dormer Stanhope, Earl of. *The Letters of Philip Dormer Stanhope, 4th Earl of Chesterfield.* Ed. Bonamy Dobrée. 6 vols. London: Eyre & Spottiswoode, 1932.

Cobbett, William. *Cobbett's Advice to Young Men and (Incidentally) to Young Women.* New York: Doyle, 1831.

Cole, G. D. H. *Samuel Butler and The Way of All Flesh*. London: Home and Van Thal, 1947.

Coveney, Peter. *The Image of Childhood: The Individual and Society: A Study of the Theme in English Literature*. Revised ed. Introd. F. R. Leavis. London, 1957; rpt. Baltimore: Penguin, 1967.

Culler, A. Dwight. "The Darwinian Revolution and Literary Form." In *The Art of Victorian Prose*. Ed. George Levine and William Madden. New York: Oxford Univ. Press, 1968.

Darwin, Charles. *On the Origin of Species: A Facsimile of the First Edition*, Introd. Ernst Mayr. Cambridge, Mass.: Harvard Univ. Press, 1964.

DeMause, Lloyd. "The Evolution of Childhood." In *The History of Childhood*. Ed. Lloyd deMause. 1974; rpt. New York: Harper, 1975.

Dodd, C. H. *The Authority of the Bible*. New York: Harper, 1929.

Epicurus. *Letters, Principal Doctrines, and Vatican Sayings*. Trans. Russell M. Geer. Indianapolis: Bobbs-Merrill, 1964.

Forster, E. M. "A Book That Influenced Me." In *Two Cheers for Democracy*. New York: Harcourt, 1951, pp. 219–23.

———. "The Legacy of Samuel Butler." *The Listener*, 12 June 1952, pp. 955–56.

Frankena, William K. *Ethics*. Englewood Cliffs, N.J.: Prentice-Hall, 1963.

Furbank, P. N. *Samuel Butler*. Cambridge, Eng.: Cambridge Univ. Press, 1948.

Gosse, Edmund. "Samuel Butler." *The Edinburgh Review*, 231 (1920), 45–62.

Grylls, David. *Guardians and Angels: Parents and Children in Nineteenth-Century Literature*. London: Faber, 1978.

Hazlitt, William. "On Cant and Hypocrisy." In *Selected Essays of William Hazlitt, 1778–1830*. Ed. Geoffrey Keynes. London: Nonesuch, 1934.

Henderson, Philip. *Samuel Butler: The Incarnate Bachelor*. London: Cohen & West, 1953.

Holt, Lee Elbert. "E. M. Forster and Samuel Butler." *PMLA*, 61 (1946), 804–19.

———. *Samuel Butler*. New York: Twayne, 1964.

Houghton, Walter E. *The Victorian Frame of Mind, 1830–1870*. New Haven: Yale Univ. Press, 1957.

Hume, David. *Dialogues Concerning Natural Religion*. Ed. Norman Kemp Smith. 1935; rpt. Indianapolis: Bobbs-Merrill, 1977.

———. *An Inquiry Concerning Human Understanding*. Ed. Charles W. Hendel. Indianapolis: Bobbs-Merrill, 1955.

———. *An Inquiry Concerning the Principles of Morals*. Ed. Charles W. Hendel. Indianapolis: Bobbs-Merrill, 1957.

———. *The Natural History of Religion*. Ed. H. E. Root. 1956; rpt. Stanford: Stanford Univ. Press, 1957.

———. *A Treatise of Human Nature*. Ed. L. A. Selby-Bigge. Oxford: Clarendon, 1888.

Jones, Henry Festing. *Samuel Butler...A Memoir*. 2 vols. London: Macmillan, 1919.

Kettle, Arnold. "Samuel Butler: *The Way of All Flesh*." In *An Introduction to the English Novel*. Vol. II. London: Hutchinson, 1953.

Keynes, Geoffrey and Hill, Brian, eds. *Letters Between Samuel Butler and Miss E. M. A. Savage, 1871–1885*. London: Cape, 1935.

Knoepflmacher, U. C. *Laughter and Despair: Readings in Ten Novels of the Victorian Era*. Berkeley: Univ. of California Press, 1971.

———. *Religious Humanism and the Victorian Novel: George Eliot, Walter Pater, and Samuel Butler*. Princeton: Princeton Univ. Press, 1965.

Lawrence, D. H. *Psychoanalysis and the Unconscious* and *Fantasia of the Unconscious*. Introd. Philip Rieff. New York: Viking, 1960.

Locke, John. *The Educational Writings of John Locke*. Ed. James L. Axtell. Cambridge, Eng.: Cambridge Univ. Press, 1968.

———. *The Reasonableness of Christianity*. Ed. I. T. Ramsey. Stanford: Stanford Univ. Press, 1958.

MacCarthy, Desmond, ed. "Charles Paine Pauli and Samuel Butler," *Life and Letters*, 7 (1931), 252–99.

Moore, G. E. *Principia Ethica*. Cambridge, Eng.: Cambridge Univ. Press, 1903.

Muggeridge, Malcolm. *The Earnest Atheist: A Study of Samuel Butler*. London: Eyre & Spottiswoode, 1936.

Plato. *Philebus*. Trans. R. Hackforth. In *The Collected Dialogues of Plato*. Ed. Edith Hamilton and Huntington Cairns. Princeton: Princeton Univ. Press, 1961.

Plumb, J. H. "The New World of Children in Eighteenth-Century England." *Past and Present*, 67 (1975), 64–95.

Pritchett, V. S. "A Victorian Son." In *The Living Novel and Later Appreciations*. New York: Random, 1964.

Shafer, Robert. *Christianity and Naturalism*. New Haven: Yale Univ. Press, 1926.

Sharma, G. N. "Samuel Butler and Edmund Burke: A Comparative Study in British Conservatism." *The Dalhousie Review*, 53 (1973), 5–29.

Shaw, George Bernard. *Back to Methuselah*. 1921; rpt. Baltimore: Penguin, 1961.

———. "Samuel Butler: The New Life Reviewed." In *The Works of Bernard Shaw*. Vol. XXIX. London: Constable, 1931, pp. 55–67.

———. *Selected Plays with Prefaces*. New York: Dodd, Mead, 1948.

Silver, Arnold, ed. *The Family Letters of Samuel Butler, 1841–1886*. Stanford: Stanford Univ. Press, 1962.

Simpson, George Gaylord. "Lamarck, Darwin and Butler: Three Approaches to Evolution." *The American Scholar*, 30 (1961), 238–49.

Stillman, Clara G. *Samuel Butler: A Mid-Victorian Modern*. New York: Viking, 1932.

Willey, Basil. *Butler and Darwin: Two Versions of Evolution*. New York: Harcourt, 1960.

———. *The Eighteenth Century Background*. London, 1940; rpt. Boston: Beacon, 1961.

———. *The English Moralists*. New York: Norton, 1964.

Wilson, Edmund. "The Satire of Samuel Butler." In *The Shores of Light*. New York: Farrar, Straus, and Giroux, 1952.

Woolf, Virginia. "A Man with a View" and "The Way of All Flesh." In *Contemporary Writers*. New York: Harcourt, 1965, 28–35.

Young, G. M. *Victorian England: Portrait of an Age*. 2nd ed. London: Oxford Univ. Press, 1953.

Zabel, Morton Dauwen. "Samuel Butler: The Victorian Insolvency." In *The Victorian Novel: Modern Essays in Criticism*. Ed. Ian Watt. London: Oxford Univ. Press, 1971, pp. 446–61.

Index